THE GLASS FLOWERS
AT HARVARD

THE GLASS FLOWERS AT HARVARD

Richard Evans Schultes

*Edward C. Jeffrey Professor of Biology and
Director of the Botanical Museum, Harvard University*

and

William A. Davis

*Keeper of Scientific Exhibits,
Botanical Museum, Harvard University*

with

Hillel Burger

*Chief Photographer
Peabody Museum of Archaeology and Ethnology, Harvard University*

BOTANICAL MUSEUM OF HARVARD UNIVERSITY

CAMBRIDGE

We humbly dedicate this book to

Leopold and Rudolf Blaschka,

creators of the Ware Collection of Blaschka Glass Models of Plants,

in appreciation of their love of nature, skill in art,

and scientific accuracy.

The Glass Flowers at Harvard

has been published in honor of the 125th anniversary

of the founding of the

Botanical Museum of Harvard University in 1858.

FRONTISPIECE: This bouquet of glass flowers was a gift to Elizabeth C. Ware and her daughter, Mary Lee Ware, from Leopold Blaschka in 1889.

CONTENTS

ACKNOWLEDGMENTS

We should like to express our gratitude to Professor Clifford C. Lamberg-Karlovsky, Director of the Peabody Museum of Archaeology and Ethnology, for placing the photographic facilities of that museum at our disposal. Our ability to overcome the difficulty inherent in photographing the models is due in large part to these outstanding photographic facilities.

We are also grateful to the authorities of the Corning Museum of Glass at the Corning Glass Center, Corning, New York, especially Dr. Dwight Lanmon, Assistant Director of Collections, who generously made available for reproduction the Blaschka work sketch of *Lilium philadelphicum*.

Finally, we wish to thank Carolyn Hesterberg for her expert typing of the manuscript of this book.

PREFACE

For many years the Botanical Museum of Harvard University has wanted a book of high-quality color photographs of its collection of glass flowers. The millions of people who have visited us continually asked if such a book was available. Until now, we have had only several pamphlets to sell at the museum. Two years ago, when Pamela Diamond, an editor at E.P. Dutton, approached us with the suggestion that we prepare such a book, we were more than pleased at the possibility of finally sharing our botanical and artistic treasure with a large reading audience that might not have the opportunity of visiting the collection.

The logistics of the operation were not difficult. Richard Evans Schultes, Director of the Botanical Museum, has been associated for more than forty years with the Ware Collection of Blaschka Glass Models of Plants. William A. Davis, Keeper of Scientific Exhibits at the museum, is intimately familiar with the models through his care of the exhibition and study of the documents concerning the manufacture and delivery of the specimens. Hillel Burger, Chief Photographer of the Peabody Museum of Archaeology and Ethnology at Harvard—sister institution of the Botanical Museum—was fortunately available for this assignment.

Although it may seem incredible to those who are aware of the complexity and delicacy of the glass flowers, the work involved in preparing this book—extricating more than one hundred models, photographing and relocating them in their cases, and writing the manuscript—was completed in the space of two months.

Throughout our labor of love, we have been assisted constantly by Pamela Diamond and her colleague Cyril Nelson. Without their guidance, suggestions, and persistence, this volume might long have languished in its period of gestation.

INTRODUCTION

HISTORICAL ASPECTS OF THE GLASS FLOWER COLLECTION

One day in 1886 an American professor set out from his hotel in Dresden with high hopes that his long journey from Cambridge, Massachusetts, would culminate in successful negotiations with two residents of this German city. Professor George Lincoln Goodale had come from Harvard University to meet with Leopold and Rudolf Blaschka, father and son partners in glass artisanship, who for some years had been producing glass models of marine invertebrates for museums all over the world.

As the first director of the Botanical Museum at Harvard, Dr. Goodale was concerned with the character of the exhibits that would be included in the museum. He was reluctant to use such available materials as dried or preserved plants and various plant products, wanting instead something that would convey the beauty and vitality of the plant kingdom and through which he could interest a large viewing audience. At that time plant replicas made of wax or papier-mâché were either crudely done or would not stand up well over a period of time. Furthermore, they did not show accurate detail.

In his determination to find the medium that would answer these problems, Dr. Goodale was following the principles laid down by Louis Agassiz who had come to Cambridge in 1846. In 1847, he accepted a Harvard professorship and soon began exerting a tremendous personal influence on the growth of science at Harvard and throughout the United States. One of his greatest desires was to establish a museum of natural history at Harvard that would serve the research needs of scientific

Dr. George Lincoln Goodale, first Director of the Botanical Museum, Harvard University. Oil portrait by Blanche Ames. *Photograph by Hillel Burger.*

Leopold Blaschka.

Rudolf Blaschka in 1913.

investigators and that could also be a means of instructing the public. His scheme comprehended a building in which all the departments of natural history would be represented. Even in his early days at Harvard Agassiz collected plant specimens and, in the limited space made available to him, gave impetus to the embryonic Botanical Museum, which dated from 1858, when Asa Gray, a Harvard botany professor, established a "Museum of Vegetable Products." Agassiz was able to see the zoological section of the museum carried nearly to completion in his lifetime. His son, Alexander Agassiz, helped to further his father's plans, which culminated in the establishment under one roof of independent museums of zoology, geology, mineralogy, and botany along with the Peabody Museum of Archaeology and Ethnology. Together they constituted what is now termed the University Museum. Throughout these developments the two chief aims were those of Louis Agassiz, which today are recognized as essential to the highest usefulness of a natural history museum: the accumulation and utilization of materials for research and the selection and display of well-presented specimens for instructing the public.

One day Dr. Goodale saw glass replicas of marine invertebrates in Harvard's Museum of Comparative Zoology (where some can still be seen on exhibit). He was convinced that this medium was the one in which a permanent botanical collection could be produced. This belief led to Dr. Goodale's journey to Dresden.

He was given a friendly welcome by the Blaschkas who listened to him politely.

The Blaschka residence at Hosterwitz near Dresden, Germany, about 1895. Leopold and Rudolf Blaschka are in the foreground.

In the course of their conversation Dr. Goodale noticed in the room several glass orchids, which had been made by the father some years earlier. This strengthened his resolve to get them to agree to make a few glass plants for Harvard.

At first the Blaschkas were reluctant to consider Dr. Goodale's proposal. To begin with, they had developed, over the years, an appreciative market for their models of marne invertebrates, which provided them with a satisfactory livelihood. In addition, the father, some years earlier, had encountered unexpected difficulties with glass models of plants that he had made not on order from anyone but merely for his own satisfaction. They were exhibited in a local museum and later were transported to a museum in Belgium. Business misunderstandings bedeviled this transaction and, after a series of involved sales negotiations, he had finally accepted a less than satisfactory monetary settlement to end the whole vexing affair. Later on, these models were destroyed when the museum burned down. After a lengthy discussion, however, Dr. Goodale was successful in persuading the two artists to agree to create a few glass models of plants for Harvard.

Although the first few models sent by the Blaschkas were badly damaged while passing through customs in New York, their excellence was such that all who saw the pieces were convinced of the appropriateness of this medium. Several Boston residents, notably Elizabeth C. Ware and her daughter, Mary Lee Ware, were struck by the beauty and excellence of the artistry and workmanship. They urged Dr.

Goodale to secure a contract with the Blaschkas, offering to finance the project. The Blaschkas agreed to produce plant models for Harvard on a half-time basis, devoting the other half of their time to continuing the production of marine invertebrates.

In the first stages of what eventually became a very extensive project, it was necessary to give thoughtful consideration to what plants should be replicated in glass, as the expected duration of the project was limited. It was thought desirable to represent as many orders, genera, and species as possible. Toward this end particular plants were chosen, and the list was sent to the Blaschkas, who used it to plan the sequence of their productions.

Some of the plants on the list were sent from America to Germany to be cultivated by the Blaschkas in their own garden and used as basic references in their work. Many of the exotic plants—particularly the tropical species—were in the royal gardens and greenhouses of the castle in nearby Pillnitz, and were made available to them for viewing.

In April 1887 the first shipment of twenty models arrived in New York. To avoid the earlier unhappy accident, prior arrangements had been made with the customs office to take the shipment directly to Cambridge, where it would be opened carefully by museum personnel in the presence of a customs official.

By 1890, while still producing plant models on a half-time basis, the Blaschkas decided that they wanted to work only with botanical models or with zoological models, but not with both. On April 16 of that same year they signed the following contract with Dr. Goodale who acted on behalf of Elizabeth C. and Mary Lee Ware.

Dresden, Saxony   April 16, 1890

This mutual agreement between Leopold and Rudolf Blaschka on the one part, and George Lincoln Goodale for the Botanical Department of Harvard University on the other part, witnesseth: that for the sum of eight thousand eight hundred (8,800) Marks payable yearly in half-yearly installments (four thousand four hundred Marks on Jan 1st and four thousand four hundred Marks on July 1st of each year) for the term of ten years from July 1st, 1890 to July 1st, 1900 by the Botanical Department of Harvard University, the said Leopold and Rudolf Blaschka do agree to make glass models of plants, flowers, and botanical details, for Harvard University in Cambridge, Massachusetts, exclusively and to engage in the manufacture of no other glass models for a term of ten years from July 1st, 1890 to July 1st, 1900. The said models of plants, flowers, and botanical details are to be sent in two (2) shipments each year. It is further agreed that the said Botanical Department of Harvard University is to defray all expenses of freight from the place of manufacture to Cambridge, of insurance, and of Consular Certificate.

The contract was signed by Leopold Blaschka, Rudolf Blaschka, and George Lincoln Goodale and was attested to by W. Knoop, U.S. Vice-Consul.

On May 12, 1890, at a meeting in Boston of the President and Fellows of Harvard College, the following letter was read:

To the President and Fellows of Harvard College,
*   My daughter Miss Mary Lee Ware and I offer, for your acceptance, a collection of glass models of*

plants, flowers and analytical details of vegetable structure, now in process of construction by the well known artists, Leopold and Rudolf Blaschka, of Germany.

A contract for the construction of the models was arranged and signed in Dresden, of April last, by L. and R. Blaschka, on the one part, and by Professor Goodale, on the other part, and meets our complete approval. We assume in full the responsibility regarding payments of the sums mentioned in the contract, and we shall provide the necessary amounts on the dates specified. It is our intention to defray all the expenses of shipment of the models to Cambridge and we shall further provide for their proper exhibition in the University Museum.

The collection was begun two years ago, and will require for its completion ten (10) years from July of the present year. It will gratify my daughter and myself if you will accept the collection as a memorial of the late Dr. Charles Eliot Ware of the class of 1834.

(signed) Elizabeth C. Ware

Boston, May 10th 1890.

    and it was

Voted that the thanks of the President and Fellows be sent to Mrs. Ware and Miss Ware for their very generous and welcome gift. Voted that the collection be gratefully accepted as a memorial of the late Dr. Charles Eliot Ware of the class of 1834.

A true copy of record
Attest:—
    E. W. Hooper
    Secy.

As their work progressed, it became necessary for the Blaschkas to examine certain tropical plants under more natural conditions. So in 1892 the younger Blaschka traveled to the Caribbean and also visited various areas of the United States, where he studied the plants of these regions, made drawings and color notes, and collected and preserved specimens to take back to the workshop in Germany for future reference. Rudolf's second field trip to America in 1895 was curtailed by the death of his father. He returned to Germany to continue this monumental project alone, a project that his father had characterized as "a first class unicum." In 1936, because of old age, Rudolf Blaschka retired from his glassworking activities.

When visitors to the museum see the delicacy of the glass flowers, they often ask how the models could possibly have been safely transported to their present location, especially from as far away as Germany.

On November 7, 1894, in a lecture delivered to the Boston Society of Natural History, Dr. Goodale expressed his belief that the packing of the flowers was "almost as wonderful as anything about them."

The Blaschkas had had years of practice in the packing of delicate objects through their previous experience in shipping glass models of marine invertebrates, and they applied the same highly successful methods to the packing of the glass flowers for shipment.

The finished model would be mounted on firm cardboard, with strong wire securing it. The mounted specimen was then placed in a sturdy cardboard box. Tissue paper was used to cushion it and keep the parts that could not readily be wired

Elizabeth C. (Mrs. Charles Eliot) Ware.

from moving. Two samples of this preparation-for-shipping technique are still on exhibit in the museum.

Next, the cardboard box would be covered; and, when a number of such boxes were ready, they were all placed in a very large, sturdy wooden box with a sufficient amount of straw padding to keep the individual boxes from touching one another or the walls of the wooden box. The wooden cover was then screwed on, and the box was embedded in more straw padding before being wrapped in burlap. The finished bale, which was nearly the height of a person, was then sent to a seaport, loaded onto a ship, and transported to America. Here, the packing procedure was reversed, much care being taken in the final process of removing the models from their cardboard boxes.

Once free of the transport package, the models were mounted on specially made plaster bases and placed in the exhibition cases. The mounting and dismounting and general care of the models were carried out for the first sixty-three years by Louis C. Bierweiler, who had come to work for the Botanical Museum in 1901. His skill in handling the models was remarkable, and his hands remained steady for this exacting task until the illness that preceded his death in 1964.

Mary Lee Ware.

Dr. Charles Eliot Ware.

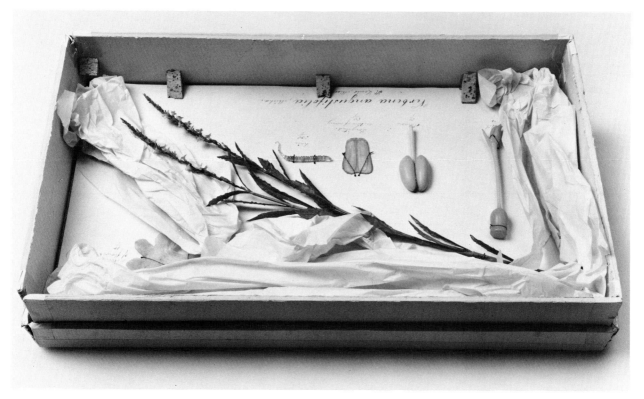

One of the original packing boxes for glass flowers shipped by the Blaschkas
to Harvard in 1894. *Photograph by Hillel Burger.*

Louis C. Bierweiler. In the foreground is the model of
Pyrus malus L. (apple).

Stories about the secret process involved in making the glass flowers have been circulating for as long as the models have been around. As early as 1889, in a letter to Miss Ware, Professor Goodale recounted various remarks made to him by the elder Blaschka as he watched the artists create the bouquet that was later presented to the Wares. Among other things, Leopold said.

Many people think that we have some secret apparatus by which we can squeeze glass suddenly into these forms, but it is not so. We have tact. My son Rudolf has more than I have, because he is my son, and tact increases in every generation. The only way to become a glass modeler of skill, I have often said to people, is to get a good great-grandfather who loved glass; then he is to have a son with like tastes; he is to be your grandfather. He in turn will have a son who must, as your father, be

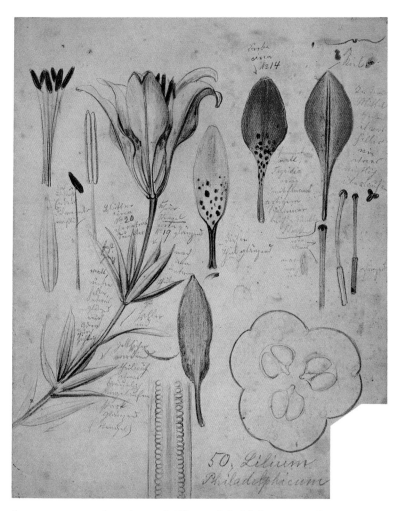

A preparatory drawing of *Lilium philadelphicum* made by the Blaschkas, *Photograph courtesy Corning Museum of Glass, Corning Glass Center, Corning, New York.*

passionately fond of glass. You, as his son, can then try your hand, and it is your own fault if you do not succeed. But, if you do not have such ancestors, it is not your fault. My grandfather was the most widely known glassworker in Bohemia, and he lived to be eighty-three years of age. My father was about as old, and Rudolf hopes my hand will be steady for many years yet. I am now between sixty and seventy and very young; am I not, Rudolf?

In the same letter to Miss Ware, he related a bit more about the modeling procedures. "The worktables," Goodale wrote,

are covered with rods and tubes of glass, and blocks of colored glass, and spools of wire of different sorts. The bellows under the table are of the ordinary sort used by glassworkers and the blast-tube is a very simple one of glass. The lamp is made of a tin cup containing a wick, and solid paraffin which melts at a pretty low temperature is used as the fuel. In making the Phlox which they asked me to bring to you and your mother, they drew first of all a rough sketch of the relations of all the flowers to each other and to the leaves, and then began to mix some glass with colors to get the right tints. The corolla is drawn and formed from a tube of glass. Then the petals are formed and melted to the tube of the corolla. The stamens are melted in next, and then the whole thing is placed in an annealing oven to remain for a few hours. It took Mr. B. just an hour and a half to make the tubes and petals of the three flowers. It required about an hour to put in the stamens and add the calyx. Next, the buds with their twists are made and all are fastened to wires covered with glass. All of these are next fastened to a stem with leaves and the product is then ready for a little paint which is added with great skill where it is required. The molding of the shapes is effected by means of ordinary pincers and tweezers. With these clumsy tools they fashion the flat plates and turn them in any way they please. With little needles fastened in handles, they make the grooves and lines and figurings of the edges. But although you may see him touch a flat piece of glass with his little metallic tools, you know that it is no ordinary touch which suddenly shapes it into a living form.

The truth, then, is that no secret process ever went into the manufacture of the models. All the techniques employed were known to glassworkers of the period. The only difference was the combination in one individual of the meticulous skill, unmatched patience, accurate observation, and deep love of the subject that the two Blaschkas brought to all of their work. These models have been described as "an artistic marvel in the field of science and a scientific marvel in the field of art"— certainly a more apt observation would be difficult to imagine.

The Ware Collection contains approximately 847 life-size models representing some 780 species and varieties of plants in 164 families, with over 3,000 detailed models of enlarged flowers and anatomical sections of various floral and vegetative parts of the plants. There are also three special exhibits: a large and selected group of the lower plants or cryptogams, illustrating the complex life histories of fungi, bryophytes, and ferns; a group of some 64 models, showing fungal diseases of fruits of the Rosaceae (apple, pear, and so forth); and, perhaps most striking of all, several exhibits of plants and insects fashioned in glass representing the different processes of pollinization. The whole collection follows the nomenclature adopted at the Gray Herbarium of Harvard University and is arranged in accord with the Engler-Gilg phylogenetic system of plant classification. The plants are exhibited by family in order of evolution, from the simplest to the most advanced or complex.

ASPECTS OF THE TECHNIQUES OF PRODUCING THE GLASS MODELS

Although the models are made almost entirely of glass, certain other materials figured in their creation. Even though we have no direct evidence in the way of records of procedures that the Blaschkas might have made during their long career as modelers of glass, we know from correspondence among the principals involved that the predominant constituent of the models was indeed glass. In some of the plant models, wire, in a variety of weights and compositions, was used to strengthen them; without the wire, models with hanging fruits or other heavy structures would have been likely to break. We know also that the glass used to make the models varied in composition and therefore was subject to variation in its working qualities. Often, to assemble successfully the many parts of a structure (or several or more structures), it was necessary that glass of varying degrees of fusibility be applied in the proper sequence. Familiarity with the wide-ranging characteristics of glass was basic to the Blaschkas' success in handling this material. Such knowledge was practically inbred in the Blaschkas from the generations of experience to which they had fallen heir.

We know also from existing letters that, in some cases, clear glass was used to create a desired shape; in other cases, colored glass was employed. When colored glass was desired, it was formed into the needed shape and, once formed, was considered finished; nothing was added to it. A reference to this aspect of the work can be found in a letter to Dr. Goodale from Rudolf Blaschka dated October 27, 1906, in which he wrote, "The Coniferae are all of self-prepared glass, nothing or almost nothing painted." His "self-prepared glass" refers to material that he had actually prepared himself: that is, which he had manufactured, using sand, alkali, and other materials in one of several furnaces installed in his studio around the turn of the century for that purpose. The reason for Rudolf's return to basics was his dissatisfaction with commercially available glass, which had gradually become inferior in quality.

When clear glass was used, it was also formed into the desired shape. To complete the work, however, color had to be applied to the surface to simulate the appearance of the original plant. Rudolf mentioned this aspect of his work in a letter to Professor Goodale on August 7, 1900:

> This is the provable fact that every model in your museum was painted by myself. I owe the knowledge of painting art to my father whose eminent gift is proved in the souvenirs I yet possess, the pictures he painted 25–30 years ago. But I got so established and versed in working very rapidly with the brush that, since more than twenty years, all and every painting of models, of the invertebrate animals as well as later of all plants came exclusively on my part.

Thus, all the plant models and marine invertebrates that the father and son produced together before 1895, the year of the father's death, were painted. Undoubtedly, many of the models that Rudolf subsequently produced by himself between 1895 and 1900 were also finished by this method, which he refers to in some of his letters as "cold painting." We do not know just when he contemplated the possibility of improving the finishing process for the models, but it must have been in the late 1890s or early 1900s. The letter above would indicate that he had not yet begun the experimental work leading to the technique that gave greater permanence to the models. His experimental work on glass through the years involved much extra effort and the investment of many hours not devoted to the actual production of the models. He spent evenings, weekends, and holidays experimenting with various glass formulas to produce his own materials, which were of the highest quality possible.

Mary Lee Ware wrote to Professor Oakes Ames, the second Director of the Botanical Museum, on the occasion of her visit to the Blaschka studio on October 3, 1928, mentioning that it had been twenty years since she had last visited the Blaschka home. Speaking of various fruit models that Rudolf had completed, she said, "One change in the character of his work and, consequently in the time necessary to accomplish results since I was last here, is very noteworthy. At that time (in the first decade of the 20th century), he bought most of his glass and was just beginning to make some, and his finish was in paint. Now he himself makes a large part of the glass and all the enamels, which he powders to use as paint." In this letter she also relates how a leaf was made, explaining that powdered glass of the proper color was applied to the surface, then heated in the flame to fuse the powdered glass to the leaf surface, thereby achieving a product that would remain unchanged.

A few samples of the material used to simulate the surface colors of some of the earlier models have been subjected to preliminary analysis: they seem to consist of a gum or glue, or a combination of both, plus mineral pigments. This material seems to respond to variations in humidity. When the humidity is high, it remains unaffected; but when the humidity falls, it becomes distorted and pulls away from the glass surface; and in some cases, it pulls fragments of glass from the underlying surface. It is possible that this movement of the coating material may be due partly to age; we simply do not know. It remains one of the mysteries yet to be solved.

The surface of some of the plant models seems unchanged. Occasionally, however, the shiny glass can be seen under an area of the applied material that has suffered from low humidity. More frequently, especially in many of the enlarged cross sections, the coating material has pulled away from the surface. As models are regularly subjected to fluctuations in humidity, the separation of this material will continue and, in time, the material will become completely detached from the underlying glass. In some of the cross sections of the ovaries, for example, the material has already become completely detached. It would therefore seen reasonable to state that on the third floor of the Botanical Museum there are more endangered species per square foot than anywhere else in the world!

Although this condition is not reversible, it can be stabilized. To halt such disintegration, the whole collection should be housed in an environment that provides constant temperature and humidity control. In the mid-1970s an attempt was made to raise funds to air-condition the halls where the collection is housed, but the fund raising for this worthy and urgent improvement has not yet been successful.

Because the glass flowers were made for Harvard, the whole collection is housed at the University. On a number of occasions, however, a few of the plant models have been exhibited elsewhere. Some were shown in Paris in 1900, but our information on this event is very sketchy. A few were put on temporary exhibit at the World's

William A. Davis, Keeper of Scientific Exhibits at the Botanical Museum, preparing the water lily model for photography. *Photograph by Oded Burger.*

Columbian Exposition in Chicago in 1893, and six models went to the Louisiana Purchase Exposition in St. Louis, Missouri, in 1904.

In 1959 Professor Paul C. Mangelsdorf, third Director of the Botanical Museum, sent six glass flowers on loan to the Corning Glass Museum in Corning, New York. Much of this museum and all six of the glass flowers were ruined in a disastrous flood in 1972. One additional model has since been lent to the new Corning Museum and is now on exhibit there.

More recently, in 1974, the fourth Director of the Botanical Museum, Professor Richard Evans Schultes, sent three models to Tokyo as part of a temporary exhibit of Harvardiana that was held at the Isetan Department Store. The three models chosen were *Camellia sinensis* (see pp. 64–65), *Panicum boreale* (see p. 22), and *Mahonia aquifolium.* As transportation has changed radically since the days of steamship travel, they were taken by plane to Japan by their present curator, William A. Davis. "Mr. Box" (the name given to the case in which the models were packed) had a seat in the first-class section—complete with seat belt and additional web belting for security—and made the whole trip by Mr. Davis's side. The three models were packed for the journey very much as they had been when first sent from Dresden to Cambridge; but instead of straw padding styrofoam was chosen as the shock-absorbing material.

Loading the glass flowers into two hearses in front of the Botanical Museum
at the start of the trip for the 1976 Steuben Glass exhibit in New York City.
Photograph courtesy Harvard Gazette.

Two years later twenty-five models were destined to make a much more difficult, albeit much shorter, trip. In early 1976 the Steuben Glass Company arranged for a special month-long exhibit of these glass flowers in their showrooms on Fifth Avenue in New York. Again it was left to Mr. Davis to supervise the packing and accompany the models.

The models, packed in wooden cases similar to those used for the trip to Japan, were to be flown from Boston to New York in a small plane. But the question of how they could be safely transported over the icy, potholed streets to Logan Airport in Boston and from La Guardia to Manhattan remained. What type of automobile had the best springs to give the smoothest ride? Although the obvious conclusion was the use of a limousine, test runs indicated a hearse was even better. So, one afternoon in March, two large black hearses, each with a driver in funereal dress, backed up to the doors of the museum, and the boxes were loaded. The automobiles proved to be such a perfect answer that, after a well-attended month-long showing, the models were not returned by air but were driven the 200 miles back to Cambridge in two hearses.

Unloading the glass flowers in New York.

The Ware Collection of Glass Models of Plants is housed in two rooms on the third floor of the Botanical Museum of Harvard University. The museum is a sturdy, New England factory-type brick building built during 1888 and 1889. The earliest shipments were stored, pending construction of the museum building, in Harvard's Botanical Garden.

The first models are now nearly a century old. When the Blaschkas began their work for Harvard, no one expected that it would go on for half a century and that such a vast collection of plants would be the result.

The glass flowers are used primarily as teaching tools in the plant sciences. Harvard University does not maintain extensive greenhouses for this purpose. If it did have such facilities, their value in teaching botany would be rather limited, because real plants flower for only a short period of time and only in their particular season. The glass flowers, on the other hand, in addition to being stunningly accurate to the smallest detail, are in flower all year round and consequently make superb teaching tools.

Over the years this collection has become a mecca for tourists, plant lovers,

The Botanical Museum of Harvard University. *Photograph by Hillel Burger.*

garden clubs, and many others. In fact, the glass flowers constitute the largest single public attraction at Harvard University, drawing over 100,000 visitors a year.

We are proud and happy to share with you the extraordinary beauty of these man-made representatives of the wonders of the plant kingdom.

THE NAMING OF PLANTS

Man has been classifying plants since recorded time. It is thought that he first classified them according to those that were useful, those that were harmful, and those that were innocuous or of no practical interest to him.

Although several ancient Greek philosophers proposed their own classifications—based either on growth habits and structure or on utility—little tangible progress was made in classical or even in medieval times.

During the Middle Ages in Europe plants were known either by their common

Harvard students Brad Jacoby and John Brown in 1976 examining specimens
in the Ware Collection of Blaschka Glass Models of Plants.

names in several languages or by long descriptive terms in Latin. There was no standardization—only chaos.

In the eighteenth century a Swedish scientist named Carolus Linnaeus created a binomial system of nomenclature; each plant had two words in its name: one for the genus, the second for the species. Thus, the potato was to be called *Solanum tuberosum* because it belonged to the large genus *Solanum;* and, as it had a tuberous underground stem, the species was called *tuberosum.* Latin was the language of science at the time, and Linnaeus published in that language. Because Latin is a dead language and therefore not subject to change, botany has retained it as its official language. For this reason, the binomials—even the names given today to newly discovered species—are Latinized.

Now, by international agreement, all nomenclature of plants takes 1753—the year in which Linnaeus published his important work *Species Plantarum*—as its official starting point. Linnaeus did more than establish the binomial system of nomenclature: he created a herbarium of dried plant specimens—now preserved in the Linnean Society of London—in which voucher specimens of most of the plants to which he gave names are still extant and available for study.

In 1753 Linnaeus wrote that the "number of plants in the whole world is much less than is commonly believed," calculating that their number "hardly reaches 10,000." But exploration, especially of tropical regions, had just begun. Nearly a century later a leading British botanist credited the plant kingdom with a total of some 100,000 species. Some botanists now estimate that the plant kingdom has 500,000 species.

Many of the plants discussed in the following pages are very well-known, cultivated species that were named by Linnaeus himself. It is for this reason that one will frequently find the abbreviation *L.* following the technical binomial. Many plants that were discovered, described, and named by later botanists or taxonomists have an abbreviation of their name appended to the technical binomial: for example, *Jacq.*, for Jacquin, an Austrian botanist of the eighteenth century. These abbreviations are not part of the plant name but are merely bibliographic aids. It is just as correct to refer to the potato as *Solanum tuberosum* as it is to call it *Solanum tuberosum* L.

As is evident in the following pages, not all plants have common names. Furthermore, the use of common names often creates problems. They may vary in the same language from one country to another; they may vary even from one part of the same country to another. The same name may be applied to different plants. Over a period of time common names sometimes change: their use may die out and new names may take their place. Common names sometimes are downright misleading: for example, "Jerusalem artichoke" refers to a sunflower with an edible, starchy tuber. It is not an artichoke; neither is it from Jerusalem! And, on occasion, what is offered in the literature as a common name is the outright invention of someone who believes that every plant must have a common name. All of this confusion and uncertainty is avoided when the accepted Latin binomial is used.

BOTANICAL ARRANGEMENT OF THE PLANTS

The glass flowers on the following pages are organized according to the most widely used botanical classification system: the Engler-Gilg system, which arranges plant families in order of their evolutionary development. Under the families, the genera, with a few exceptions, appear alphabetically in this book.

THE GLASS FLOWERS

Taxus canadensis *Marsh*
Ground Hemlock

Taxaceae
Yew Family

The yew family, which has eight species in one genus, is native to the Northern Hemisphere. The evergreen shrubs or small trees are very branched with scaly, reddish brown, resin-filled bark and linear, usually two-ranked resinous leaves; the fruit consists of a bony seed embedded in a fleshy, cup-shaped scarlet aril. Several species are grown as ornamentals and are planted widely in Europe, especially in cemeteries. The wood of *Taxus* is used to make cabinets and archery bows. All species of *Taxus* are poisonous, containing toxic alkaloids known as taxine in the foliage, bark, and seeds. The plant is toxic to man and all kinds of livestock. In England, where yew is widely planted, it is considered to be the most dangerous of all poisonous shrubs.

Taxus canadensis, native to northeastern America, is one of the popular horticultural species. A straggling shrub, rarely taller than 60 inches, it has several horticultural varieties. Despite its toxic character, *T. canadensis* is reputedly used in Quebec as an antirheumatic.

Panicum boreale *Nash*   Gramineae
Panic Grass   Grass Family

The Gramineae is undoubtedly the world's most important economic family. All cereals are grasses; the family also supplies fiber, sugar, essential oils, thatching materials, alcohol, starch, fats, and one of the bases for the plastic industry. There are 620 genera and some 12,000 species of grasses that grow throughout the world in almost every habitat but are sparse in the humid tropical forests. Most species are herbaceous, annuals or biennials or long-lived perennials. The treelike bamboos may live 120 years. Their sharply distinguishing characteristics (especially in the way they grow) set them apart from other plant families: their intercalary meristem or nodal, instead of a terminal, growing point, their fibrous root system, their stems with prominent nodes, their narrow leaves with sheathing bases, small flowers in spikelets, and dry, one-seeded fruit or caryopsis. Notwithstanding their diminutive size, grass flowers are beautifully complex. More than 80 genera of grasses are cultivated domestically.

Some of the most noble grasses are members of the 500-species genus *Panicum,* which is found worldwide in tropical and warm temperate zones. The spikelets of *Panicum* are two-flowered. They are annual or perennial herbs. A few species are cultivated, especially the several millets, which are of local importance as cereals in India and parts of Africa.

Panicum boreale, a wild grass native to the northern half of North America, is slender and erect, attaining a height of about 20 inches. The leaf sheaths are stiff and hairy along the margin. The leaf blades are approximately 5-inches long and are somewhat hairy along the base. The flowering stalk, or panicle, is loosely flowered; the spikelets are finely pilose. In the late summer the plant branches sparingly from all of its nodes. This grass grows mostly on riverbanks and in moist ground or in woods.

Collinia elegans (*Mart.*) *Liebm.*   Palmae
No common name known   Palm Family

The Palmae are known as Principes (princes of the plant kingdom). They represent one of the economically most important families, with some 2,800 tropical and subtropical species in 217 genera. Palms are a characteristic feature of tropical vegetation in both hemispheres. They are woody shrubs, vines, and trees: the arborescent condition is not common in the monocotyledons. They vary from giant trees that reach 200 feet to a species that matures at 18 inches. In the tropics palms are second only to the grasses (to which they are related) in their utility to man. In addition to their ornamental value, palms are the source of many useful products: waxes, fats, oils, edible fruits, starch, sugar, alcohol, fibrous materials for ropes, brooms, basketry, thatch, hats, and mats; one Amazonian species furnishes vegetable ivory; and the tender young shoots ("palm hearts") of some species are used as food.

Three species of *Collinia* are native to Central America. These palms are delicate, shade-loving, reedlike forest plants growing singly or in clusters with multiple trunks. They are closely related to *Chamaedorea* and were formerly included in that genus.

Collinia elegans is a dainty palm attaining a height of about 48 inches with slender trunks measuring about 1 inch in thickness. The many-branched flowering stalks have pale yellow unisexual flowers—the male and female are on separate plants—and bear small orange-red fruits. It is commonly planted in pots for ornamental purposes indoors: in fact, it is the most popular cultivated palm for shopping centers and hotel lobbies.

Ananas comosus *(L.) Merr.*
Pineapple

Bromeliaceae
Pineapple Family

The Bromeliaceae, native to tropical America, comprises more than 1,600 species in some 60 genera. Most species are epiphytic, although some are terrestrial or grow on rocks. The greatly reduced stem produces a rosette of fleshy or leathery leaves forming pitchers that are usually full of water and organic debris and that give rise to a spike or head of flowers with often very brightly colored bracts. Many bromeliads are now cultivated as ornamentals.

Undoubtedly, the most important economic genus is *Ananas* with its five tropical American species, including the pineapple. *Ananas comosus* is derived probably from the wild *A. ananasoides,* which still grows wild in the Amazon, although it has been suggested that the species was domesticated in Paraguay by the Tupí-Guaraní Indians. By the time North America was discovered, the plant had diffused to Mexico and the West Indies. After 1492 the pineapple rapidly spread throughout the tropics, undoubtedly valued by seamen as a preventative against scurvy. It is a perennial that will bear fruit for fifty years. It can be reproduced by slicing the "crown" off the top of the fruit and planting it. The edible portion of the fruit is made up of swollen carpels. Modern cultivars are devoid of seed. Some of the superior varieties of pineapple are grown by the Indians of the northwestern Amazon.

Eichhornia azurea *Kunth*
Water Hyacinth

Pontederiaceae
Pickerel Weed Family

The pickerel weed family is composed of erect or floating herbs. The family includes some 30 species in six genera, which grow usually in the tropics of both hemispheres. The most commonly recognized species is the pickerel weed, *Pontederia cordata,* which is native to North America but has been naturalized in Europe. The species of this family have no economic use other than as ornamentals.

Seven species of *Eichhornia* occur in nature from the southeastern United States south to Argentina and the West Indies. The plants root at the nodes and have floating or immersed leaves. The floral spikes are conspicuously erect. Two species are grown horticulturally.

Eichhornia azurea has beautiful flowers that are lavender-blue with a deep purple center and often yellowish markings. The flowers are showy but last only a few hours. *Eichhornia azurea* has shoots that may reach 72 inches in length from their roots in the mud. Reproduction is by means of stolons, or horizontal stems, that give rise at the tip to a new plant. A related species, *E. crassipes,* multiplies so rapidly that in many parts of the tropics it has choked rivers and streams and become a serious threat to navigation.

Lilium canadense *L.*   Liliaceae
Meadow Lily   Lily Family

The Liliaceae, one of the largest families with 250 genera and at least 3,700 species, is cosmopolitan but is found in great concentrations in temperate and subtropical regions. It is outstanding as an ornamental family. Most species are perennials; rarely are lilies annuals. They are usually herbs, but a few tropical forms become shrubby or treelike. At the end of each season most species die back to a bulblike organ or rhizome. Many are xerophytic; some are fleshy. The flowers are usually showy and brightly colored. A great number of species with showy flowers are important as ornamentals: some 60 genera with one or more species are cultivated for their horticultural value. Economically, lilies yield a few foods; some are fiber plants, and a significant number serve as medicines or poisons.

The 80 North Temperate species of *Lilium* are erect, leafy-stemmed herbs with scaly bulbs and usually showy flowers with terminal stalks. At least fifty species are of horticultural importance.

Lilium canadense is an American species attaining a height of 36 to 48 inches. It grows from Quebec and Nova Scotia south to Alabama. The pendant flowers, which number up to sixteen, are yellow or orange bell-shaped with ¾-inch dark spots. There are several named varieties, differing from one another primarily in their floral coloration.

Yucca filamentosa *L.*   Agavaceae
Adam's Needle   Agave Family

The Agavaceae, a segregate from the Amaryllidaceae, or amaryllis family, has approximately 670 species in twenty genera. The species are woody—even tree- or vinelike. Perhaps the best-known plant of the family is the widely cultivated *Agave americana*, the American aloe or century plant. The species are all of American origin. The economically important species in this family are the pulque plant, the cantala, the henequen, the istle, the sisal, and the Mexican maguey.

Yucca is a curious group of xerophytic plants, comprising about 40 species that grow in the southern United States, Mexico, and the West Indies. They are all striking plants, are stemless, and reach the height of small trees, have stiff, bayonet leaves and showy, hanging or erect clusters of white, cream, or violet, waxy cup-shaped flowers. Several species—at least seven—are commonly cultivated as ornamental curiosities. Some species—especially the Joshua tree (*Y. brevifolia*)—yield steroidal sapogenins for the preparation of medically important cortisone and estrogenic hormones. Most species of *Yucca* have developed a mutual dependency and adaptation of their flowers to a single species of insect for pollination. The flowers emit a fragrance at night, which attracts the small moth that effects pollination.

The leaves of *Yucca filamentosa*, as the species name indicates, yield a fine and strong fiber. The species is native to the eastern part of the United States and is widely grown in gardens as an ornamental. The stem arises from a running rootstalk and bears leathery leaves measuring 18-inches long that are spiked at the tips. The flowers are densely borne on a pyramidal cluster that can grow as high as 72 inches. Each flower is large and creamy white.

Iris versicolor *L.*   Iridaceae
Iris; Fleur-de-Lis   Iris Family

The iris family comprises ninety genera and at least 1,200 species and grows in the temperate and tropical regions of both hemispheres. Most of the cultivated species are herbaceous with showy, bisexual flowers. The name *Iris* comes from the Greek word for "rainbow"; the name was given to the flowers because of their many colors.

The more than 300 species of *Iris* are found mainly in the North Temperate Zone. At least 60 species are cultivated, but there are hundreds of horticultural varieties and strains, or races, of named cultivars. The plants have bulbous or creeping rootstocks, and the stems bear one or several swordlike leaves. Many species have highly fragrant and showy blossoms.

Iris versicolor, a fertile hybrid thought to be the product of two very similar species that were crossed in antiquity, is native to northeastern North America. The 42-inch-high stems arise from stout rhizomes. The leaves may reach a length of 36 inches. The delicate blue to violet flowers arise from a membranaceous, green leaflike spathe: the falls, or outermost segments of the flower, are obovate and 3-inches long, the haft yellow-green verging into a bright yellow blotch on the violet-blue blade; the standards, or inner floral segments, are almost spoon-shaped and are a rich violet-blue.

Musa rosacea *Jacq.*
No common name known

Musaceae
Banana Family

The Musaceae comprises five genera, all tropical and native to Africa, Asia, and Australia. They are often gigantic herbs with branching rhizomes, or underground creepers, giving rise to large leaves with sheaths that curl inside the bud and form what appears to be a stem or trunk; the trunk may vary in thickness. Some species can attain a height of 15 feet or more. Their large flat leaves, with stout midribs, are among the largest leaves in the plant kingdom. Their flowers, several to many, usually have brightly colored bracts or spathes; they are often rich in honey and are visited constantly by birds and bees. The family is important as the source of ornamentals and of food and fiber plants. Some members of this family are among the largest of all herbaceous plants: included in this family are the traveler's palm, bird-of-paradise, and Heliconia.

Musa is an Old World genus of 50 or more species of rapidly growing treelike herbs with large, spirally arranged leaves that—together with their sheathing bases—make up a trunk. The flowers are borne in clusters on long spikes that are usually drooping and are enclosed in colored bracts. The important species of *Musa* are *M. paradisiaca* (plantain), *M. paradisiaca* var. *sapientum* (banana), and *M. textilis* (Manila hemp).

Native to India, *Musa rosacea* is a small member of the genus. It reaches a height of 72 inches with leaves that are 36-inches long and 12-inches wide. The drooping flowering spike measures 12 inches, and the delicate bluish bracts under the flowers grow to approximately 8 inches in length. Its yellow-green fruit is not edible.

Laelia crispa *Reichb. f.*
No common name known

Orchidaceae
Orchid Family

The Orchidaceae is the largest family of plants with some 30,000 to 35,000 species in over 700 genera. Terrestrial and epiphytic (on rare occasions, saprophytic) perennials with tubers or pseudobulbs, they are cosmopolitan but are especially abundant in the tropics. The family is distinguished by having a gynandrium, or column: the union of style, stigma, and stamens. One of the three petals on each flower is usually enlarged and altered, often drastically so, into a lip, or labellum, a landing place for insects. Most species have one stamen, but some have two. Few plants have so complexly adapted themselves to insect pollination as the orchids. Representatives of 50 or more genera are cultivated as ornamentals. Hybrids, numbering in the thousands—many of which are bi- or plurigeneric—are prized by horticulturists. The only major economically valuable species is *Vanilla planifolia*, the source of commercial vanilla.

The 30 species of *Laelia*, a relative of *Cattleya* with which genus they hybridize easily to form the horticulturally important group *Laeliocattleya*, are native to tropical America, growing primarily in Mexico, Guatemala, and southern Brazil. They are pseudobulbous epiphytes with long fleshy or leathery leaves and showy blossoms borne singly or in pairs or in many-flowered spikes. The lip of the flower is usually three-lobed. *Laelia* has long been a horticultural favorite.

The Brazilian species *Laelia crispa* has pseudobulbs that grow up to 10-inches long. The leaves attain a length of 12 inches, and the flowering stalk, which gives rise to five or six handsome, highly fragrant blossoms that are 6-inches wide, is equally long. The plant is named "crispa" because of the beautifully waved and crisped petals. The side lobes of the lip are rounded and white, and are yellow with reddish streaks at the base; the midlobe is deep purple and conspicuously waved.

Odontoglossum grande *Lindl.*
Baby Orchid; Boca de Tigre; Uña de Gato

Orchidaceae
Orchid Family

One of the most spectacular groups of the orchids is *Odontoglossum,* a genus of some 200 species that is native to Mexico, Central America, the West Indies, and tropical South America. Many species are planted for greenhouse cultivation, but half a dozen have become outstandingly important to horticulture. The flowers are showy, with a wide range of colors and much variation in size and shape. One of the characteristics that endears them to growers is the long-lasting nature of the flowers.

The baby orchid is a beautiful, large-flowered species with (in nature) long flowering-stalks with very large (5 to 6 inches in width) yellow blossoms that have cinnamon-brown crossbars; the lip of the flower is yellow or whitish. This species, native to Guatemala, is the member of the genus with the largest flowers. It has been extensively crossbred to produce valuable and highly variable hybrid forms of great beauty.

Odontoglossum crispum *Lindl.*
No common name known

Orchidaceae
Orchid Family

Native to the mountains of Colombia, *Odontoglossum crispum* is an extremely variable species that has been crossed extensively with other species of the genus to produce many horticulturally valuable hybrids. The beautiful flowers are prolific. The flattened pseudobulbs measure about 3 inches in length, the two leaves on each pseudobulb reaching 12 inches in length. The many flowers are borne in a panicle, or elongated cluster, that may be 24-inches long or more. The flowers, which measure up to 3½ inches in width, are white, variously crimson- or brown-spotted, occasionally rose-tinted or yellowish; the lip is fringed, with a deep yellow throat; the column is oddly shaped, resembling a bird with a sharp beak and spreading wings. The beauty of the flowers lies perhaps in the combination of their large size and their delicate colors and texture.

Salix cinerea *L.*
Ashy Willow

Salicaceae
Willow Family

The Salicaceae includes the aspens, the poplars, and the willows. Centered primarily in the North Temperate Zone, the trees, shrubs, and subshrubs of this family—530 species in three or four genera—have unisexual flowers borne on different plants in erect or drooping clusters called aments, or catkins. The flowers are highly reduced, with no petals and usually no sepals. The seeds are covered with long, silky hairs.

The genus *Salix* has 500 species of trees or shrubs, although some arctic species are almost herbaceous and prostrate. Hybridization in nature is common, and many species are difficult to identify as a result.

Many species of willow, such as the weeping willow (*Salix babylonica*), are grown as ornamentals; most cultivated forms are of hybrid origin. A few have supple, withy twigs and are used in basketry, especially the cultivated osier (*S. viminalis*); the bark of some has been employed in tanning (because of the high tannin content) and in medicine (as a source of salicylates).

Salix cinerea, the common ashy willow, has a soft, silky catkin, which flowers just before the leaves appear and is prized as a harbinger of spring.

Bougainvillea spectabilis *Willd.*
Bougainvillea

Nyctaginaceae
Four-o' Clock Family

The four-o' clock family is made up of thirty genera and about 300 species of herbs, shrubs, and trees. It is native to warm climates and is especially numerous in the Americas. The flowers vary greatly, but they usually have basal bracts that often are large and colored. The family includes some ornamentals, but otherwise it has little economic significance.

Bougainvillea, with 18 species, is native to tropical South America. Robust, showy vinelike shrubs, they owe their spectacular beauty not to the flowers, which are small and insignificant, but to large, brightly colored leaflike bracts that may be red, purple, orange, or white. The genus is named for Louis de Bougainville, the first Frenchman to navigate the Pacific Ocean. When he stopped to replenish his supplies in Rio de Janeiro, he had a botanist on board collect specimens, which were introduced into France in 1768.

A number of horticultural varieties of *Bougainvillea spectabilis* have white, cream-colored, or salmon-colored bracts. The three bracts enclose densely hairy, inconspicuous flowers, which are usually greenish. The plant is easily grown from cuttings in wet, sandy soil.

Nymphaea odorata *Ait.*
Fragrant Water Lily

Nymphaeaceae
Water Lily Family

Perennial water plants, the members of the Nymphaeaceae (including those species sometimes treated as a separate family, the Nelumbonaceae) are cosmopolitan and are comprised in some 80 species in eight genera. The leaves are mostly large and simple, arising from a long, leathery leafstalk, which in turn rises from a stout and erect, or branched and creeping, rootstalk. The usually bisexual flowers float—or sometimes stand—high above the water. They may have any number of petals. Water lilies were well known to man in ancient societies: he saw in their blossoms the promise of purification and regeneration. These flowers have been venerated in many religions of the Old World and the New, and there is some evidence that certain species in both hemispheres may have been used as sacred hallucinogens. Water lilies had former economic significance: the seeds, which contain starch, oils, and proteins, were an emergency food in Europe, Africa, and Asia. During the Middle Ages some water lilies were used in medicine.

The main genus of the family is *Nymphaea,* which includes about 40 species growing in temperate and tropical regions and many horticultural hybrids. Floral color runs the whole spectrum from white, cream, and yellow to coffee color, pink, bloodred, crimson, bluish, violet, and purple. Most species have flowers that open during the day; tropical species usually open in the late afternoon and remain that way all night.

Nymphaea odorata, as its species name indicates, belongs to a section of the genus in which the flowers are extremely fragrant. This species is native to eastern North America, where it is commonly seen in its usual white-flowered form and where, on Cape Cod, a pink-flowered type occurs in the wild. A form with larger white flowers is found in the southern parts of North America and in the American tropics. This horticulturally important species has contributed to the creation of many hybrids.

Aconitum columbianum *Nutt.*
Monkshood; Wolfsbane

Ranunculaceae
Crowfoot Family

The crowfoot family, with perhaps 1,500 species of herbs in 50 genera of temperate and cool climates in both hemispheres, has many poisonous and medicinal species. The family is also noteworthy, however, as the source of many ornamentals. Some species, like the buttercup (*Ranunculus acris*), have become weedy.

At least eight of probably 100 species of *Aconitum* are important cultivated plants—as sources of medicinal compounds or as ornamentals. All species are attractive, with their racemes of blue or purple—or sometimes white or yellow—flowers with five petallike sepals, the uppermost petals being hooded or helmet-shaped. The most commonly cultivated medicinal species is *A. napellus,* source of the drug aconite; it is a European species.

Aconitum columbianum, a species of the western part of the United States and Canada, is likewise toxic; it is frequently cultivated as an ornamental. The common name monkshood refers to the hoodlike uppermost sepal that gives the flower such a bizarre appearance. The roots of the plant were once considered to be poisonous to wolves, hence the plant's other common name, wolfsbane.

Anemone patens *L.*
Pasqueflower

Ranunculaceae
Crowfoot Family

The 150 species of *Anemone* are cosmopolitan, growing mostly in the North Temperate Zone or in high mountains. They are spring-, summer-, or autumn-flowering species—perennial herbs with rhizomes and radical leaves. The plants do not exceed 24 to 36 inches in height. Some 24 species are cultivated for their beautiful flowers.

Anemone patens is a soft-hairy plant that grows up to 6 inches in height. The daisylike flowers are usually violet, and measure 2 to 3 inches in width. The species is native to Europe and northern Asia, but there is a very close variety—sometimes considered a distinct species—peculiar to North America from the Midwest to British Columbia and stretching into Siberia.

Hepatica triloba *Chaix*
Liverleaf

Ranunculaceae
Crowfoot Family

The ten species of *Hepatica,* a genus native to the North Temperate Zone, are low perennial herbs with leaves borne on thickened petioles. The generic name *Hepatica* and the common English name liverleaf come from the leaf's liverlike shape.

    Hepatica triloba is native to Europe and northern Asia, but a very close variety—sometimes considered a distinct species—is peculiar to North America, growing in woods from Nova Scotia south to Florida and west to Minnesota. The six to twelve flowers are blue, purplish, or white. It is one of the most welcome signs of spring in New England forests. It differs from the closely allied European species, *H. nobilis,* in that it is less hairy; it also has smaller flowers. In the Middle Ages the plant was thought to be a cure for jaundice and other liver complaints because of the shape of the leaf.

Dendromecon rigida *Benth.* Papaveraceae
Bush Poppy Poppy Family

The Papaveraceae, with 200 species in 26 genera, is found chiefly in the North Temperate Zone of both hemispheres. It has given many species to horticulture but is best known for the opium poppy (*Papaver somniferum*), source of morphine, the bane and blessing of humanity. The species are usually herbs, rarely shrubs. Most of them contain a milky white latex. At least thirteen genera are important ornamentals. The poppies of garden importance belong to several genera.

This genus is perplexing: some botanists consider that there is one polymorphous species; others recognize twenty. Most modern students believe that there are two species: one Californian, one Mexican. The name *Dendromecon* means "tree poppy" in Greek.

The so-called bush poppy occurs in the drier parts of the California coastal hills. It is a shrub that ranges in height from 24 to 120 inches and has a distinctive whitish bark. The juice is not milky. The leaves are leathery. The flowers, which are solitary and terminal, measure 2-inches wide and are golden yellow.

Romneya coulteri *Harvey*
Matilija Poppy

Papaveraceae
Poppy Family

Romneya, a genus of two Californian and northwestern Mexican species, is an erect perennial herb or small shrub. Both species are planted for their showy flowers.

   Romneya coulteri, native to southern California, attains a height of 48 to 96 inches. The plant is profusely branched. The leaves are blue-green, leathery, and 2- to 4-inches long. The white flowers, which remain on the plant for many days, measure 6-inches wide and are exceedingly fragrant (whereas the flowers of the only other species have a disagreeable scent); they are notable because of their dense mat of numerous yellowish stamens.

Dionaea muscipula *Ellis*
Venus's-Flytrap

Droseraceae
Sundew Family

Of the four genera of this curious family, only *Drosera*—the sundews—is cosmopolitan. The family is especially numerous in Australia and New Zealand. The ten species of the family are herbs found usually in acidic bogs; the leaves are borne in basal rosettes and are glandular-hairy and insectivorous.

The genus *Dionaea* has only one species—*D. muscipula*—and it has a very restricted geographical range: damp, mossy places in the pine barrens of North and South Carolina. However, it is much sought as an odd pot ornamental. The plant has a rosette of extraordinary leaves: each leaf has a winged petiole functioning like a normal leaf, an upper kidney-shaped blade with a hinged midrib and long hairs along the margin, and three sensitive trigger hairs on each lobe; when touched, these blades close, and the hairs are basally jointed so that they fold down when closing occurs. Insects thus entrapped are digested by secretions from glands on the leaf surface. The famous naturalist Charles Darwin, who wrote the treatise *Insectivorous Plants,* called Venus's-flytrap "the most wonderful plant in the world."

Nepenthes sanguinea *Lindb.*
Pitcher Plant

Nepenthaceae
Nepenthes Family

The two genera of this curious carnivorous family of pitcher plants have some seventy species that grow in the Seychelles Islands, in tropical Australia, on the Malay Peninsula, and in New Caledonia. Many are herbs. Some are woody, erect or climbing plants that are frequently epiphytic. The tendrils, which aid the plant in climbing, are extensions of the midrib of the leaves. The ends of the tendrils are greatly expanded and hollowed and may develop into a colored pouchlike pitcher with two fringed or hairy wings; the edge of the pitcher is curved inward and has honey glands that attract insects, which are then drowned in the water collected in the pitcher and are eventually digested.

The most important genus, *Nepenthes,* has 67 species, with many artificially produced horticultural varieties. The pitchers—red, wine-colored, cream, or greenish with violet or purple spots—often become very large, in some species measuring as long as 7 inches, but on occasion reaching 18 inches in length; one species may develop pitchers as long as 36 inches. The genus first attracted attention in 1658, when the French botanist Étienne de Flacourt described a species from Madagascar; and it was later said to be the only species from Ceylon, where it was called a "vegetable wonder." They grow in moist environments, from sea level to 10,000 feet. 10,000 feet.

Nepenthes sanguinea has, as its species name indicates, a reddish pitcher. It is native to Malaya and has been used in creating hybrids, although its cultivation is difficult. This species was introduced to horticulture in England in 1849.

Echeveria secunda *Booth*   Crassulaceae
No common name known   Orpine Family

A very natural family, the Crassulaceae comprises 1,500 species in thirty-five genera of herbs of cosmopolitan distribution but largely concentrated in South Africa. Most species are perennials with extremely fleshy leaves and a waxy surface in a tufted arrangement, typical of many plants that grow in dry, rocky habitats. Many species are horticulturally very important as "succulents," grown inside or under glass, or in pots, rock gardens, or along borders.

Echeveria grows in the New World from the southern United States to the northern Andes. Perennials, the 200 species of this genus are distinguished by flowers with erect, thick, and fleshy petals that spread only at the tips and are united at the base. The leaves, which grow in dense rosettes, are broad and flat.

Echeveria secunda (often known as *Cotyledon secunda*) has no stem; it produces stolons, or underground shoots, that produce new young plants. The leaves are erect and light green with a sharply pointed red tip. The flowering stalk produces from ten to twenty-four red blossoms. This species, now widely grown as an edging or border plant, is native to Mexico.

Fragaria vesca *L.*   Rosaceae
Strawberry   Rose Family

The Rosaceae represents one of the large plant families, with some 2,000 species in 100 genera. It includes trees, shrubs, and herbs, is cosmopolitan, and usually perennial. The family is a major contributor to horticulture, with species of importance belonging to some 45 genera. Many of the most popular temperate zone fruits are rosaceous: strawberries, apples, pears, crab apples, quinces, loquats, medlars, plums, almonds, apricots, cherries, peaches, blackberries, dewberries, raspberries, loganberries, and others.

Strawberries are the most important small fruits of the temperate zone. The fruit is not a berry but an aggregate fruit consisting of many small achenes, or dry fruits, embedded in the flesh of a receptacle. Strawberries have been cultivated in Europe since the fourteenth century. They were introduced into North America by the early English Colonists. Their importance as a cultivated crop in the United States dates from 1860. There are three main sources of our cultivated strawberries, but hundreds of varieties of these three types exist.

Fragaria virginiana, the early eastern North American type, is the kind that was cultivated by the early American settlers and taken to England. *Fragaria vesca* is a European species, source of all of the ever-bearing kinds. The large modern cultivated forms are all of hybrid origin, descendants of *F. chiloensis,* a small, wild form native to the coast of South America, and *F. virginiana.* Their crossing took place in a nursery in Paris and set in motion a great resurgence in the consumption of strawberries as a dessert fruit.

Pyrus malus *L.*   Rosaceae
Apple   Rose Family

There is some confusion over the nomenclature of the apple. It is sometimes called by the technical name *Malus sylvestris* and at other times *M. pumila.* Whether it is included in the genus *Pyrus* or in *Malus* depends essentially on the point of view of the botanist; the main difference rests in the presence of stone cells in the flesh of the fruit in *Pyrus* and their absence in *Malus.* The approximately 45 species of *Pyrus,* all trees, are native to temperate Europe, Asia, and North America. In addition to numerous ornamental species the genus has such important fruits as the crab apple, the Chinese pear, the snow pear, and the pear.

Undoubtedly the most important fruit in temperate regions, the apple is native to eastern Europe and western Asia. It has been cultivated for over 3,000 years, and apple seeds have been identified in the Swiss Lake Dweller remains dating back 4,000 years. The classical Romans knew 22 types of apples; today, 6,500 "varieties" exist, thanks to the variability of the progenitors of the cultivated apple and to the mutability and ease of hybridization of the group.

The early Colonists imported the apple to North America, and by 1750 there were many orchards in the English Colonies. Today, although apples can be grown from seed, they are usually propagated by grafting or budding. Because of all the fruits apples keep the best, they were a favorite fruit until the present century for people in cold climates, who could eat them fresh throughout the winter. This characteristic, in addition to the fact that their juice can be turned into cider and vinegar, made apples the most popular and most utilized of all temperate fruits. The apple has a number of other uses: applejack, an alcoholic beverage prepared from cider; apple concentrate, apple powder, apple pomace, apple syrup. This last product is used to maintain proper moisture content in bread, cigarettes, and smoking tobacco.

The fruit of the tree of knowledge mentioned in Genesis, quite generally considered to be an "apple," could not have been our apple. More probably apricots were the fruit indicated. Although some students believe that the term means "oranges," this citrus fruit, native to China, was unknown to Asia Minor when the biblical episodes are presumed to have occurred.

Prunus persica *(L.) Batsch*   Rosaceae
Peach   Rose Family

In its broadest classification there are more than 400 species of *Prunus* (about 50 of which are cultivated). The genus is cosmopolitan. Some 25 to 30 species are native to North America. The genus includes the well-known stone fruits: cherries, plums, almonds, and apricots. All are small trees with white or pinkish bisexual flowers, sometimes borne singly but usually in clusters.

The peach, or *Prunus persica,* is native to China but was once believed to have originated in Persia, hence the species name. The small tree is short-lived. The pink flowers, which appear before the leaves unfold, measure ½ to 2 inches in width. Several distinct varieties—the nectarine and the flat peach—are of commercial importance. Between 2,000 and 3,000 varieties are known. The stone of the fruit is typical, reddish, very hard, and conspicuously pitted. The peach is the second most important fruit in the United States. It was known in the Mediterranean region in classical times, and by the Romans who recognized six "varieties."

Brownea rosa-de-monte *Berg*
Scarlet-flowered Brownea; Rosa de Monte; Palo Cruz

Leguminosae
Pea Family

One of the largest and most cosmopolitan plant families, the Leguminosae comprises some 12,500 species in 600 genera. On the basis of the type of flower, the family is divided into three subfamilies: Mimosoideae, Caesalpinioideae, and Papilionoideae. The Leguminosae have a typical fruit: a pod or legume that characteristically opens along two sutures, or edges. The family has great economic significance. The seeds of many species are protein-rich foods; many species are valuable fodder plants. The family yields fine woods, fibers, dyes, tannins, oils, waxes, gums, resins, narcotics, poisons, medicines, spices, and perfumes; in fact, there are few categories of useful products in which the legumes are not important: no legumes are sources of rubber or caffeine-rich species. The roots of many species have nodules with bacteria that are capable of forming nitrates from atmospheric nitrogen, thus enriching, instead of impoverishing, the soil.

Some two dozen species of *Brownea,* growing as shrubs or small trees, are native to tropical America and the West Indies. The young shoots appear with soft rolled-up pinkish leaves that hang down until they mature, turn green, and assume their normal positions.

Some species, like *Brownea rosa-de-monte,* have large, showy round heads of scarlet or reddish flowers. Because of the color of the flowers, Amazonian Indians believe that sawdust from the wood and bark of the plant has hemostatic properties that, when applied to wounds, hastens the coagulation of the blood.

Mimosa pudica *L.*
Sensitive Plant; Humble Plant

Leguminosae
Pea Family

The genus *Mimosa* comprises about 350 species of trees, shrubs, and herbs, which grow chiefly in the American tropics but include a few species native to Asia and Africa. The species have delicate, twice-pinnate leaves and tiny flowers in dense heads or spikes. Many species of *Mimosa* are thorny or prickly. Most of the so-called mimosas of nurseries are species of *Acacia,* especially *A. armata.* Some species are employed as cover crops or as a source of firewood. *M. hostilis,* a Brazilian species, has been used by Indians as the source of a hallucinogenic drink.

   Mimosa pudica is a slightly woody plant that became famous in Europe shortly after 1492 because of its sensitive leaves, which close up upon contact and "go to sleep." It was rapidly introduced into the tropics, where it became a familiar plant, often growing wild. Its leaves are long-petioled and have many linear-oblong segments that are about ¼-inch long; old plants develop conspicuous prickles on the stems. In addition to being a natural curiosity in horticulture, *M. pudica* has acquired pseudomedical importance in Java, where bits of the plant are placed in the bed of a restless child to induce sleep, an example of sympathetic magic.

Erythrina crista-galli *L.*　　　　　　　　　　　　　　Leguminosae
Cockscomb; Cockspur; Coral Tree　　　　　　　　　　　　Pea Family

The genus *Erythrina* comprises mostly woody species, many of which are large trees with showy—usually red—flowers. The 100 species, some of which are grown as ornamentals, are tropical and subtropical, native to both hemispheres. Many species have toxic alkaloids in the seeds, which are often highly colored, generally red. Some species are grown as shade trees on coffee plantations.

The cockscomb, a Brazilian species, is a shrub or small tree; it is the most frequently cultivated species in the warmer parts of the United States. The beautiful, waxy crimson flowers, which are borne on long terminal stalks, attain a length of 2 inches. The common name cockspur comes from the stout backward-bent spines on the petioles, while the technical name *crista-galli* ("cockscomb") and the English cockscomb come from the broad, conspicuous standard, or main petal, of the large red flowers.

Lathyrus splendens *Kellogg*
Pride of California

Leguminosae
Pea Family

The genus *Lathyrus* includes some 130 species, annual and perennial herbs and small shrubs native to the Northern Hemisphere and the cool mountains of South America. At least 10 species are major horticultural plants, including the popular sweet pea (*L. odoratus*) and the everlasting pea (*L. latifolius*). One species has tuberous roots that provide a food like the potato; several are grown in Mediterranean Europe as fodder or as the source of beans that are eaten like chick-peas.

Lathyrus splendens, as its common name indicates, is native to southern California. A slender, low shrub growing to several feet in length, this species has beautiful flowers, angled stems, and branched tendrils. The leaflets occur in three to five pairs; and the leaves are borne on long magenta-red stalks. The pod has a prominent beak. This species is one of the rarer garden ornamentals, but its beauty warrants its greater utilization as an ornamental perennial.

Euonymus atropurpureus *Jacq.*
Wahoo; Burning Bush

Celastraceae
Staff Tree Family

The 850 species of the Celastraceae in 55 genera occur in both the tropics and temperate zones of both hemispheres. Most species are trees or shrubs, often climbing ones. The family is distinctive in that most species have small greenish flowers and brightly colored arils on the seeds. Members of six genera are cultivated, but the only major useful plant in the family is kat (*Catha edulis*), a shrub, the leaves of which are chewed in Arabia and adjacent areas of northeastern Africa as a habituating stimulant.

The largest genus of the Celastraceae is *Euonymus* with species of shrubs and trees that grow in the North Temperate Zone, especially in the Himalayas, China, and Japan. Some species are poisonous. Twelve or fifteen are horticulturally important, primarily because of attractive leaves—turning red in the autumn in some species—and red fruit.

Euonymus atropurpureus has finely toothed elliptic leaves, purplish flowers, and a deep scarlet four-lobed fruit with brownish seeds with a bright scarlet aril.

Acer rubrum *L.*   Aceraceae
Red Maple; Scarlet Maple; Swamp Maple   Maple Family

One of the most conspicuous families of the north temperate and tropical mountain regions is the Aceraceae, which consists of trees and shrubs in three genera. There are 200 species, many in China and Japan. Fifteen species are native to the United States and Canada.

Some species of *Acer* have a watery, often saccharine sap. The sugar maple (*Acer saccharum*) of eastern North America is exploited commercially, yielding two to four pounds of maple sugar per tree in February and March, the months of tapping. Many species are grown as shade trees or for their ornamental foliage. Some yield excellent timber and firewood. The fruit of the family is characteristically made up of two nutlets, or samaras, with an elongated wing on one side.

Acer rubrum, the red maple, may grow to a height of 120 feet. The twigs are reddish. The red flowers appear long before the leaves unfold in the spring. In the autumn the bright scarlet foliage offers a show of unbelievable beauty in the landscape of the northeastern United States and eastern Canada. Several varieties grow in more southerly parts of the United States. *Acer rubrum* was introduced into England from Virginia by John Tradescant II as early as 1637.

Gossypium herbaceum *L.*
Levant Cotton

Malvaceae
Mallow Family

The Malvaceae comprises approximately 1,000 species in 75 genera that grow in the tropics and temperate zones of both hemispheres. The family is noted mainly for ornamental and fiber-rich species. The flowers are usually showy, with numerous stamens united at the base, forming a staminal tube or column.

According to contemporary studies the genus *Gossypium* comprises about 20 species, four of which are economically important as sources of the cotton fiber, hairlike outgrowths of the seeds. Cotton was known to the ancients in both hemispheres: there are many references to it in classical Greek and Roman writings, and it was known in India as early as 1800 B.C. The cottons had several independent origins, for the Mexicans and Peruvians had cotton fabrics long before 1492. The cotton-yielding species of *Gossypium* have been very drastically altered by millennia of domestication, selection, and hybridization.

Most of the cotton of the United States is produced by *Gossypium barbadense* and *G. hirsutum,* both native to the New World. Levant cotton (*G. herbaceum*), a herbaceous annual forming a subshrub up to 54-inches tall, is probably native to southwestern Asia and is Asia's chief cotton plant. It is believed to have contributed to the hybrid origin of some of the American short-staple cottons.

Hibiscus clypeatus *L.*   Malvaceae
Congo Mahoe   Mallow Family

Between 250 and 300 species of *Hibiscus,* herbs, shrubs, and trees grow in the temperate and tropical areas of both hemispheres. Numerous species are extensively cultivated in the warmer regions as ornamental hedge plants. Their flowers are large, mostly bell-shaped, and are usually brightly colored. The genus is noteworthy as the source of many ornamental species; at least 20 occupy places of importance in horticulture.

    Hibiscus clypeatus is a velvet-hairy shrub that can grow up to 15 feet in height and is native to the West Indies. It grows in open arid woodlands, thickets, and along limestone seashores. The flowers, which measure up to 2½ inches in width, are a dull tawny yellow tinged and lined with red inside; they grow redder with age.

Camellia sinensis *L.*   Theaceae
Tea   Tea Family

The tea family comprises 500 tropical and subtropical trees and shrubs in eighteen genera. The leaves are often glossy and leathery. Eight or ten genera are in cultivation as ornamentals or as economic products. The genus *Camellia* has 80 or more shrubby species, native to tropical and subtropical Asia.

Native to southeast Asia, tea in nature is a tree that often grows to 30 feet in height but under cultivation remains a 3- or 4-foot shrub. It is a true *Camellia* but was formerly called *Thea sinensis*. Like the cultivated ornamental camellias, it has glossy, leathery leaves and beautiful fragrant flowers. Tea leaves are gathered from new or young shoots produced by the constant pruning of the shrub. One thousand varieties of the tea plant have been developed. Production varies from 200 to 1,000 pounds an acre, and a single plant may yield for fifty years or longer. Tea is the most popular of the caffeine beverages, used by more than half the world's population. Its stimulant effects are due to the caffeine content (1 to 4 percent); its astringency is due to tannins; its flavor to polyphenols and essential oils—the proportions varying with the age of the leaves, the method of processing, and the variety of tea. Originally valued as a medicine, tea came to be used as a beverage in China around A.D. 600. It was introduced into Europe in the sixteenth century but did not become important until the late seventeenth century. China, India, and Ceylon produce 85 percent of the world's tea.

Passiflora laurifolia *L.*
Jamaica Honeysuckle; Yellow
Granadilla; Water Lemon

Passifloraceae
Passion Flower Family

The passion flower family is predominantly tropical American, comprising some 600 species of shrubs and herbs in about a dozen genera. The name of the family comes from the belief among early European explorers of America that the complex flower symbolized elements of the Crucifixion: the fringe of the flowers representing Jesus' crown of thorns; the petals and sepals standing for the ten faithful apostles; the five stamens indicating Christ's five wounds; and the three knoblike stigmas depicting the nails.

The important genus of this family is *Passiflora,* with 500 species primarily in tropical America but with a few in Asia, Australia, and Madagascar. They are all climbers. Several species have edible fruits.

One of the favorite ornamentals is *Passiflora laurifolia,* which is native to tropical America. A stout climber, it has flowers measuring 4 inches in width that are white with reddish spots and a crown that is equal in length to the white-banded violet sepals. The fruit, known as the water lemon, is edible.

Carica papaya *L.*
Papaya

Caricaceae
Papaya Family

This strange family of four genera and 55 species of tropical America and Africa is made up of small, soft-wooded "trees." The straight trunks have a terminal crown of large palmate or digitate leaves. They are monoecious or dioecious and usually have a milky juice.

The 40-some species of *Carica* are all native to the New World except one, which is native to Africa. They are small "trees"—actually giant herbs—with a fleshy, erect trunk. The fruits are fleshy berries. All have a milky juice.

The papaya is now widely grown in tropical and subtropical regions for its delicious melonlike fruit, a fleshy orange-yellow berry that may weigh up to twenty pounds. The flowers are a clean, waxy white. The latex contains a digestive ferment, papain, which helps digest proteins. For this reason *Carica papaya* is used in medicine and as a meat tenderizer.

Cereus aethiops *Haworth*
No common name known

Cactaceae
Cactus Family

The familiar family of succulents, the Cactaceae, has some 140 genera and at least 2,000 species, usually of the warmer or even desert areas of the New World from Canada south to Argentina. Many species have been introduced into the Old World, where they are now growing wild, but one genus, *Rhipsalis,* may be native to Africa. All cactus plants exhibit adaptations for the conservation of water. They vary greatly in nature, having fleshy, cylindric, globular, or flattened, often jointed, stems generally armed with spines and glochids (barbed bristles). The flowers are often large, showy, and colorful, with many stamens. Several species in at least 40 genera have become horticultural favorites; some yield edible fruits; a few are narcotic or poisonous, or are employed in native medicine.

Cereus is a South American and West Indian genus of some fifty usually treelike species that give a weird effect to the desert landscape. The flowers are usually funnel-shaped, large, nocturnal, cream or white, and borne simply along the lengths of the stem. Most species are tall and much branched with angled or ribbed and spiny branches.

Native to Argentina and Brazil, *Cereus aethiops* is bushlike, with its profuse branches and rounded, spiny, bluish green or purplish ribbed stems. It can reach a height of 72 inches. The flowers, which are 9-inches long and 5-inches wide, have a rose-colored exterior and white interior perianth segments. The ovoid or elongate-ovate fruit measures 2½-inches long and turns brown when it is ripe.

Echinocereus engelmannii *(Parry) Ruempl.*　　　　　　　　　　　　　　Cactaceae
No common name known　　　　　　　　　　　　　　　　　　　　　Cactus Family

The sixty species of *Echinocereus* are usually low-growing cacti that may stand erect, lie prostrate, or hang. They are native to the dry regions of the southwestern United States and northern Mexico. The funnel-shaped, red, purple, or yellow flowers are large and attractive; consequently, a half dozen or so species have been introduced into horticulture as succulents. The globose or cylindrical stems are densely clustered, ribbed, several-jointed and are usually very spiny. The variously colored fruits are frequently edible.

　　Echinocereus engelmannii of California, Arizona, Utah, and adjacent Mexico forms large clumps of shiny stems with joints 4- to 12-inches long and spines ½-inch long; the central spines, which are stout and twisted, attain a length of 2 inches. The flowers are purple and 3-inches long. This cactus is a favorite house plant.

Opuntia stanlyi *Engelm.*
Prickly Pear

Cactaceae
Cactus Family

This typical and well-known cactus genus has at least 300 species that occur from southern New England (where it probably was introduced) west to British Columbia and south through Central and South America to southern Patagonia. Although some species have gone wild in the drier parts of the Old World, the genus is strictly American. Many species are grown by cactus fanciers; several yield edible fruits; some are planted as hedges to fence in cattle. The species vary greatly in size and habit, from prostrate plants under 6 inches to branching trees with trunks. The stems and branches are flat or rounded, usually with very fleshy joints. The flowers vary in color from green to red and yellow.

Native to our Southwest—New Mexico and eastern Arizona—and Mexico, *Opuntia stanlyi* has low stems—usually shorter than 20-inches high—that branch profusely; the joints measure about 7 to 8 inches in length. The numerous, long, stout spines are very conspicuous. The yellow flowers measure 2½- to 3-inches wide; and the spiny yellow fruits are equally long. This species has become an ornamental favorite.

Eucalyptus globulus *Labill.*   Myrtaceae
Blue Gum; Tasmanian Blue Gum   Myrtle Family

The myrtle family, with 3,000 species of woody plants in about 100 genera, grows primarily in tropical America and especially Australia. The family is characterized by glandular-punctate leaves and a great number of stamens. Many species are valued as ornamentals; a few are the source of hardwoods; some yield edible fruits; several are spice plants.

Eucalyptus, with an estimated 500 species, most of which are Australian (several native only to Indomalaysia), has been widely distributed in cultivation around the warmer parts of the world. Because of its rapid growth, it is very frequently planted as a wood source.

Eucalyptus globulus has scythe-shaped leaves and yields a colorless, spicy, pungent oil that is used in medicine as a decongestant. It is cultivated in California, the Mediterranean, and the Andes, but the tree has the disadvantage of desiccating the soil because of its height and extensive root system.

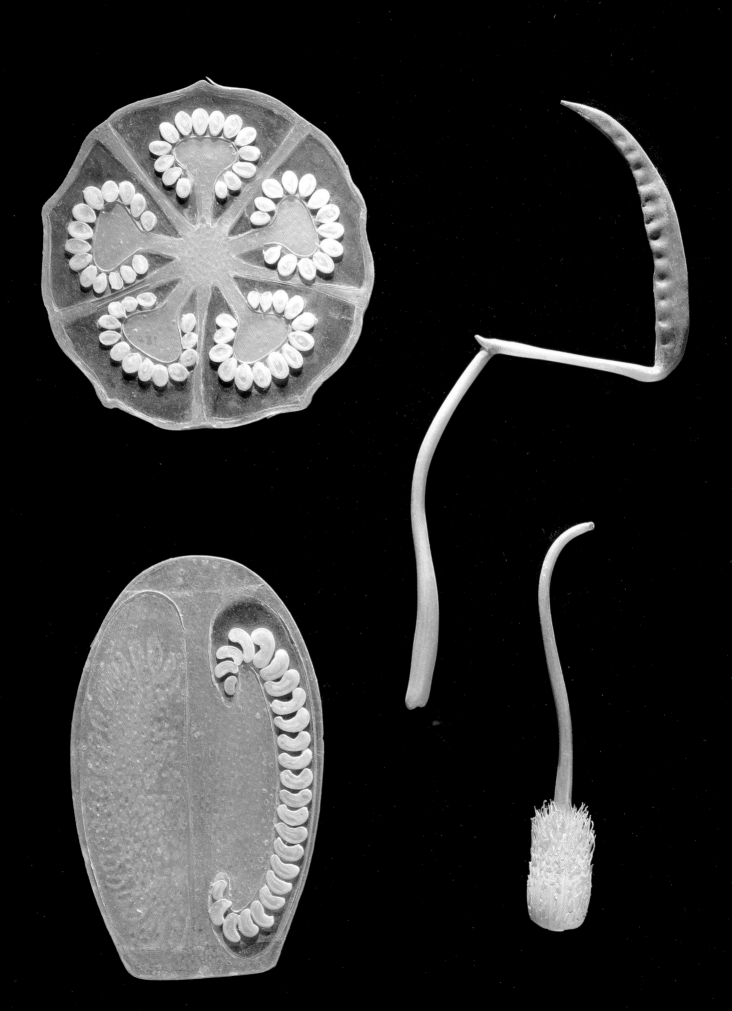

Tibouchina semidecandra   Melastomaceae
(Schrank et Mart.) Cogn.   Melastoma Family
Glory-Bush

Mainly a tropical family, the Melastomaceae has an estimated 3,000 species and some of the most striking ornamentals of the plant kingdom. It is one of the easiest families to recognize, with its typical leaf venation (most species have three main veins that are much more conspicuous than the others) and the usually geniculate (bent sharply at an angle) stamen. Beyond their ornamental value the family is of little economic use, although there are some species that yield dyes. The Melastomaceae is richly developed, especially in the Amazon Valley.

Representatives of some ten genera have been introduced into cultivation. One of the most important is *Tibouchina,* a genus of about 200 species.

Tibouchina semidecandra, native to Brazil, is notable for the showy violet to reddish purple flowers that measure 3- to 5-inches wide. The common English name, glory-bush, is derived from the spectacular appearance of this 48- to 120-inch-high shrub when it comes into full bloom.

For the 4 enlarged parts on the opposite page:
Upper left: Transverse section of ovary.
Lower left: Longitudinal section of ovary.
Upper right: Stamen, showing geniculate, or knee-shaped, form typical of this family.
Lower right: Pistil.

Punica granatum *L.*
Pomegranate

Punicaceae
Pomegranate Family

This interesting but tiny family has one genus and two species. It is native from the Mediterranean to the Himalayas. Because of its cultivation as a fruit, one species, the pomegranate, is widely distributed. The family has become adapted to tropical and subtropical regions.

Punica granatum—source of the pomegranate—is a deciduous shrub or small tree that grows up to 20 feet. The orange-red flowers become a bright red or yellow fruit the size of an orange and have the form of the crown of persistent sepals that, according to legend, was the inspiration for a royal crown. The many white seeds are embedded in a crimson or pink acid pulp, giving rise to the medieval belief that the pomegranate was medicinally effective against diseases of the mouth and gums. The plant is native to southern Asia but has become naturalized throughout the Mediterranean area. A dwarf variety has been developed for hothouse cultivation.

There are twenty-eight references to the pomegranate in the Bible, including its importance in the erection of the Temple of Solomon. Even today, people in the Mediterranean countries believe that pomegranates protect against evil spirits, and wreaths of pomegranate flowers are hung around children's necks to relieve stomach ills.

Lopezia coronata *Andr.*
No common name known

Onagraceae
Evening Primrose Family

The Onagraceae comprises mostly perennial herbs (with a few shrubs or trees) and is native to tropical and temperate areas of both hemisphers; it is especially abundant in North America. Some species are aquatic. The family is composed of 21 genera and some 650 species. Many species have become favorite ornamentals.

Lopezia, native to Mexico and Central America, has 15 or more species. Despite the bright colors and the curious structure of the flowers, the genus is rarely cultivated. The species are erect undershrubs or herbs. The usually small flowers have two stamens attached to the pistil: one anther bearing, the other a sterile, petallike staminode. There are nectaries at the base of the flower, and these attract insects.

The beautiful pink, rose-colored, or lilac flowers of *Lopezia coronata* are borne singly in the leaf axils of the upper half of the stem. The plant is an annual that reaches a height of 36 inches. The two upper petals are linear, the laterals broader and longer. The fertile stamen has an upward tension, the staminode a downward tension: this causes an explosion when an insect enters the flower.

Kalmia latifolia *L.*   Ericaceae
Mountain Laurel; Calico Bush;   Heath Family
Spoonwood

The heath family is nearly worldwide, except in very dry areas, and is most numerous in cool, moist mountainous regions of the tropics. It is made up of more than 1,500 species in 70 genera. Most are woody and range from undershrubs to stout shrubs and small trees; some species are epiphytic.

A few species of *Vaccinium* have edible fruits, such as blueberries, huckleberries, and cranberries; the root of an *Erica* is used in making briar pipes; wintergreen oil is derived from *Gaultheria*. A number of species are toxic. Members of 27 genera are cultivated as ornamentals or economic plants.

Eight species of *Kalmia* are native to North America and Cuba. They are evergreen, rarely deciduous, shrubs with bright green leathery leaves and showy flowers, usually in terminal heads. The genus is named for the famous Swedish botanist Peter Kalm who, as a student of Linnaeus, traveled and collected in America in the late eighteenth century.

Kalmia latifolia, the famous mountain laurel of the northeastern United States, is usually shrubby but may become treelike. It is a common ornamental along New England highways. The foliage is richly dark green on both surfaces. The rose-colored to white flowers with purple markings have a mechanism that explodes and sheds the pollen on honey-seeking insects, which carry the pollen immediately to another flower. A native of eastern North America, *Kalmia latifolia* is the state flower of Pennsylvania. A dwarf variety, with leaves only 1- to 2-inches long, has been developed for horticultural use.

Monotropa uniflora *L.*
Indian Pipe

Ericaceae
Heath Family

Monotropa is a curious saprophytic genus having two species that are devoid of chlorophyll and live on decaying organic matter, much in the manner of mushrooms. This genus is sometimes included in the Pyrolaceae or the Monotropaceae. There are five species of the North Temperate Zone, mostly occurring in pine, birch, and beech forests. The underground, branched root system has fungal mycorrhiza that help nourish the plant from organic matter in the soil. All are low, fleshy herbs that are tan, red, or white with stems that spring from a cluster of fibrous mycorrhizal rootlets. Attempts to cultivate *Monotropa* as a curiosity have never met with success.

The Indian pipe (*Monotropa uniflora*) is an evanescent, snow-white, erect herb that may attain a height of 9 or 10 inches. It has one nodding flower (as its technical species name, *uniflora*, indicates). The plant, on drying, turns black. *Monotropa uniflora* grows throughout temperate North America and recurs in Japan and the Himalayan regions. *M. coccinea*, a beautiful scarlet species, grows in the mountains of southern Mexico.

Rhododendron maximum *L.*
Great Laurel; Rosebay

Ericaceae
Heath Family

The 600 species of *Rhododendron* are almost all native to the temperate zones of both hemispheres, with the greatest concentration of them growing in eastern Asia, especially in the Himalayas; there are more than 250 species in Malaysia alone. They are stout evergreen shrubs or small trees, usually with leathery leaves and tubular or funnel-shaped flowers in bunches. The rhododendrons are probably our most prized shrubby ornamentals in the cooler parts of the United States and Europe.

The great laurel, native to eastern North America from Nova Scotia to Georgia and Alabama, is one of the showiest of the 600 species of *Rhododendron*. It has beautiful dark green leaves and rose-colored flowers that are spotted green and white inside. The spots are 1½-inches wide and occur in many-flowered clusters in late spring or early summer. This species, together with *R. catawbiense* of the southern Appalachians, is the parent of many hardy hybrids. Most cultivated rhododendrons today are hybrids.

Jasminum sambac *Ait.*
Arabian Jasmine

Oleaceae
Olive Family

The 600 species in 29 genera of oleaceous plants are cosmopolitan, but are concentrated in temperate and tropical Asia. They comprise trees and shrubs, several of which are grown as ornamentals. This family is the source of olive oil.

Jasminum is a genus of 200 species of climbing or erect shrubs that is entirely Old World. The species with white flowers are fragrant; those with yellow flowers are without any aroma. Several species are cultivated for their essential oil, which is extracted for use in the perfume industry.

Arabian jasmine, or *Jasminum sambac,* climbs to a height of 60 inches and has angular, hairy branchlets. Native to India, this species has white flowers that measure up to 1-inch wide and grow in clusters of a few to many blossoms. This is one of the more than fifteen species that are cultivated as ornamentals.

83

Gentiana andrewsii *Griseb.*
Closed Gentian

Gentianaceae
Gentian Family

There are 900 species in 80 genera in the gentian family. It has been one of the most popular families in horticulture, used especially in rock gardens. The family occurs in all parts of the world and in many ecological zones. Some are arctic and alpine plants, saprophytes (living on decaying organic material like mushrooms), and halophytes, which grow along salt coasts and in bogs. They are perennial or annual herbs, or in some cases, shrubs. The funnel- or bell-shaped flowers tend to be bluish.

At least 30 of the 400 species of *Gentiana* are commonly grown in temperate gardens, although cultivation often poses problems. It has been said: "If a Gentian will thrive with you, you cannot go wrong with it; if it doesn't thrive, not all the King's horses nor all the King's men will induce it to do so." Most are tufted alpine perennials or annuals. They are common in nearly every cool or high area, except in Africa. Gentians form one of the strikingly beautiful features of the Alps. In addition to being used as ornamentals, gentians are sometimes valued as medicines, especially the yellow-flowered *G. lutea,* which is the source of a stomach tonic: the roots, which are dug in the autumn, then sliced and dried, contain a glycoside.

Gentiana andrewsii is a 24-inch-high perennial with ovate-lanceolate leaves that are 4-inches long, and deep blue flowers that grow in terminal clusters. The corolla of this species is closed at the tip, not open as in most species. The plant is native to eastern North America from Quebec south to Georgia.

85

Asclepias curassavica *L.*
Bloodflower

The milkweed family, the members of which produce a milky latex, has some 2,000 species in 130 genera, all native to the tropics and subtropics of both hemispheres. They are erect or twining herbs or shrubs. The flowers are complex in their structure and function: the stamens and carpels are united into a complex organ called a gynostegium, and the pollen is usually united into masses called pollinia that are carried from one flower to the next on the legs of insects, transferred to the insect by an organ known as the translator. Some of the species are toxic, one species being an active ingredient in a South American arrow poison; one African species is used as a fish poison.

The 150 species of *Asclepias,* the majority of which are native to Africa and North and South America, are perennial herbs. Several species have been cultivated.

The beautiful *Asclepias curassavica,* or bloodflower (the name refers to its reddish or orange flowers), is native to tropical America, where it frequently becomes a weed. It attains a height of 36 inches and has terminal or axillary bunches of flowers, each flower measuring about ¼ inch in width. The corolla is reddish or purplish red; the hood, orange.

Calotropis procera *L.*
Akund

Asclepiadaceae
Milkweed Family

Calotropis is a small genus of half a dozen tropical species of fleshy shrubs that are native to the drier parts of Africa and Asia.

Two species—*Calotropis gigantea* and *C. procera*—are so similar that there is some doubt that they are distinct. Both have seeds that produce a kapoklike silk-cotton fiber and a small amount of drying oil. The copious sticky latex is highly resinous. In India, *C. procera* is considered to be medicinally valuable in treating intermittent fevers, dysentery, leprosy, elephantiasis, syphilis, and rheumatism. It contains an alkaloid that acts on the heart muscle.

Ipomoea hederacea *(L.) Jacq.*
Morning Glory

Convolvulaceae
Morning Glory Family

The morning glory family, with 55 genera and 1,650 species in the warmer parts of both hemispheres, is made up of mostly twining annual or perennial herbs, but it has a few erect herbs and even trees and shrubs. Some species have a milky juice; a few have tuberous roots. The flowers are usually large, funnel-shaped, and beautifully colored. There are few convolvulaceous plants of economic value; several are potent hallucinogens; several are medicinal purgatives. The sweet potato belongs to this family.

Ipomoea, with 500 species, is found in the tropical and warm temperate parts of both hemispheres. Most species are vinelike herbs or shrubs; a few are aquatic or strand plants. The genus has provided some of our most prized garden ornamentals, and there are many horticultural hybrids in the group. At least 15 species are major cultigens. *Ipomoea* is economically noteworthy as the source of jalap root, a purgative derived from the roots of several species, and of the sweet potato.

The beautifully blue- or purple-flowered *Ipomoea hederacea* is a slender, hairy annual with small ovate or heart-shaped leaves. The flowers are small for the genus (up to 2-inches long) but make up for any horticultural loss from their size in the delicacy of their coloration.

Phlox ovata *L.*
Mountain Phlox

Polemoniaceae
Phlox Family

The Polemoniaceae is a family of 15 genera and 300 species of mostly annual or perennial herbs with a few woody members. Although most species are North American, the family has representatives in Europe, South America, and northern Asia. Many species are grown as ornamentals for their beautiful flowers. The leaves are usually hairy. The five stamens are attached to the inside of the corolla tube.

Phlox, the well-known genus of garden plants, has some 50 species of annuals or perennials that grow in temperate regions: all but one species (which is Siberian) are native to North America. They hybridize easily, and many beautiful hybrids have transformed the usually modest flowers into the glorious cultivars that are now so highly prized as ornamentals.

Phlox ovata, which grows in open woods in mountainous areas from Pennsylvania south to Alabama, is unusual in the genus in not being densely hairy. A perennial, it attains a height of 20 inches with leaves 4 inches in length. The flowers are distinctly stalked in close bunches, are 1-inch wide, and vary in color from pink to pale red or purplish. Phlox blossoms in late June and July.

Phacelia minor *Thell.*
California Bluebell

Hydrophyllaceae
Waterleaf Family

The waterleaf family, with 18 genera and about 250 species that grow worldwide (but are especially concentrated in North America), counts many ornamentally valuable members. The leaves are usually radical, normally hairy, and often glandular. The flowers tend to be blue or purple and to secrete a nectar attractive to bees. The species are usually herbs, rarely shrubs.

Phacelia has 100 species of annual or perennial herbs that are native to America. The flowers are borne on a scorpioid inflorescence: a flowering stalk coiled so that it resembles the tail of a scorpion.

One of the horticulturally important species is *Phacelia minor,* which is native to southern California, a loosely branching annual that attains a height of 24 inches. The plant is hairy throughout. Its bell-shaped, blue or purple flowers measure ¾ inch in width and are covered with sticky, glandular hairs. A strain with white flowers has been developed.

Monarda didyma *L.*
Bee Balm; Fragrant Balm; Oswego Tea

Labiatae
Mint Family

The Labiatae, a very large family that is worldwide, with its principal center of diversity in the Mediterranean, has more than 3,500 species in 180 genera. Most species are herbs or undershrubs, but a few are small trees; included in the family are many xerophytic species that have adapted to dry or even desert conditions, some bog plants, and a few vinelike members. The mints are relatively easy to recognize: the stems tend to be square; the usually zygomorphic or uneven flowers are bell- or funnel-shaped with two lips; and the leaves often have epidermal glands that secrete volatile oils. Many species are of horticultural value, but it is the essential oils that make the family of economic importance as the source of condiments (peppermint, spearmint, thyme, oregano, pennyroyal, and others) and perfumes (rosemary, lavender, patchouli).

The genus *Monarda* has a dozen species of erect, tall, aromatic annual or perennial shrubs with dense heads of large white, red, purple, or yellow flowers that are often mottled. The flowers are visited by bees (hence the common name bee balm) and hummingbirds.

Monarda didyma is native to North America, growing in moist woods from Quebec to Michigan and south to Georgia. This plant is a popular and easily grown garden species, a robust plant with a profusion of scarlet flowers that are 2-inches long. Several varieties with purplish or violet, pink or rose, crimson and white flowers have been developed. The leaves of this and other species are thought to have medicinal properties and are used in folk medicine as a tea (hence the common name Oswego tea).

91

Salvia patens *Cav.*   Labiatae
Gentian Sage   Mint Family

The more than 700 species of *Salvia* grow in the tropical and temperate zones of both hemispheres. A large number of species are grown as ornamentals; some are cultivated as medicinal or culinary plants: the well-known sage is *S. officinalis.* The species vary: they may be annual, biennial, or perennial herbs, subshrubs, or shrubs. *Salvia* has developed a complex pollination system in which an insect hits one end of an elongated portion of the stamen that bars access to the nectar, which forces the other end of the stamen down and brushes the insect's back with the pollen.

Salvia patens, a perennial that grows 12- to 30-inches high, has soft, arrow-shaped leaves and slender spikes of large beautiful blue flowers that measure up to 2 inches in length. It is valued as a bedding or a conservatory plant. The species is native to the mountains of Mexico.

Brugmansia arborea *(L.) Lagerh.*   Solanaceae
Angel's-Trumpet   Nightshade Family

The nightshade family, with more than 2,000 species in 90 genera, is the source of some of our most important economic plants: potato, tomato, tobacco, chili pepper, eggplant, and a number of poisons, medicines, and narcotics. The family, which is notable as being one of the richest in alkaloids, is made up of herbs, shrubs, and small trees. It is nearly worldwide in distribution but has its main center of diversity in the Andean regions of South America.

The genus *Brugmansia,* which has ten species, is very closely allied to *Datura.* All species are arborescent; all are known only through cultivation; all are highly poisonous; all are native to South America, especially the Andes; all species contain high concentrations of alkaloids. Many are widely used in folk medicine in primitive societies of South America and, despite their dangerous toxicity, are taken as sacred hallucinogens by the Indians.

Brugmansia arborea (more frequently known as *Datura arborea*) is native to the high Andes of Colombia, Ecuador, and Peru. The original specimen was collected a century ago in Peru by the Spanish botanists Ruiz and Pavón. It is a shrub or small tree, usually under 12 feet in height. The young branches and leaves are clothed with soft white hairs. The flowers, which have a musklike odor, are white and trumpet-shaped, measure up to 9 inches in length and flare at the mouth, which is divided into five teeth separated by distinct sinuses or notches. Several of the other white-flowered species of *Brugmansia* have been incorrectly called *B. arborea. Brugmansia arborea* is a rare species in the field but has been introduced into cultivation.

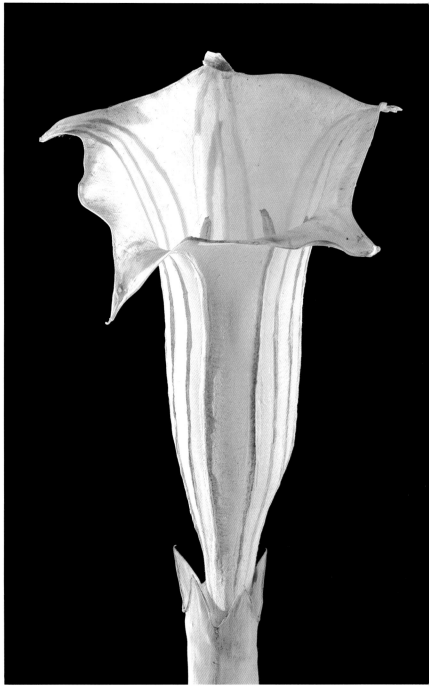

Solanum tuberosum *L.*   Solanaceae
Potato   Nightshade Family

Solanum is one of the largest genera of the plant kingdom, with upward of 1,700 species growing in the temperate and tropical zones of both hemispheres; they are herbs, shrubs, often trees, sometimes vines; many are toxic because of the alkaloidal content of most parts of the plants. In addition to the potato, the genus has other economically valuable species: the Jerusalem cherry (*S. pseudo-capsicum*), the Peruvian pepino (*S. muricatum*), the eggplant (*S. melongena*), and the bittersweet (*S. dulcamara*). Very closely allied to *Solanum* (and sometimes included in it) is *Lycopersicon*, the genus of the tomato (*L. esculentum*).

Undoubtedly, the most important species of *Solanum* from the viewpoint of human history is the potato. The tuber-producing species belongs to a small segment of the genus, including some 170 species, 10 of which have had a role in the evolution of the cultivated potato. It is native to the temperate Andes. Because many wild potatoes are toxic, early Andean agriculturists must have selected less toxic clones; this took place as early as 5000 to 2000 B.C. The presumed wild species that were the progenitors of modern potatoes still grow in the Andes.

Before the discovery of America potatoes had not reached Mexico or other parts of North America. The Spaniards first introduced the plant into Europe in 1537. It was introduced into England 50 years later. The first potatoes came to North America from England in 1621. It took 200 years for the potato to achieve any agricultural importance in Europe. It first became popular in Ireland because the cool damp summers favored growth of the crop, while cereals were difficult to cultivate. It was not until the end of the nineteenth century that modern potato types began to appear. Great changes are expected in potato breeding and evolution during the next several decades, as scientists strive to shape the crop to meet modern needs. One of the trends of the future may be to adapt the crop to cultivation in truly tropical regions.

Nicotiana glauca *Graham*
Tree Tobacco

Solanaceae
Nightshade Family

The genus *Nicotiana* consists of 21 Australian and Polynesian and 45 North and South American species. They are usually herbs, although a few, like *N. glauca,* become shrubby or arborescent. All species are annuals or perennials of warm regions. Whereas the most important species economically are *N. tabacum* and *N. rustica,* which are grown for tobacco and for use as an insecticide, a number of others have become horticultural favorites because of their beautiful bearing and showy flowers.

    Nicotiana glauca belongs to the same section of the genus as *N. rustica.* A rapidly growing shrub or small tree reaching a height of 20 feet, it has thick, rubbery leaves that, when young, have a bluish bloom similar to that of *Eucalyptus* hence, the species name *glauca.* It is native to Argentina but has spread throughout tropical and subtropical America. Several "varieties" of *N. glauca,* differing primarily in leaf shape, have been described, but they seem to be merely ecological variants. The foliage is considered to be toxic to cattle, horses, and sheep; the leaves contain an alkaloid called anabasine that is more efficacious than nicotine in killing aphids. Notwithstanding its common name, *N. glauca* seems not to have been smoked as tobacco by native peoples.

Pentstemon spectabilis *Thurber.*
Beardtongue

Scrophulariaceae
Figwort Family

The figwort family, very important as the source of ornamentals, has some 3,000 species in 220 genera. Most species are herbs or subshrubs, with only a few that are shrubs or trees; a few are also climbers. They are widely distributed. The family is distinguished by its zygomorphic or irregular tubular flowers. The family is not economically important, save for its ornamental species and for being the source of the valuable heart medicine digitalis.

    Pentstemon is a genus of 250 or more species, all of which are native to North America, chiefly the western areas of the United States. They are perennial herbs or shrubs. The genus is characterized by having four functional stamens and usually a bearded staminode (a sterile stamen). About 50 species have been introduced into horticulture.

    Pentstemon spectabilis, which attains a height of from 24 to 72 inches, has 3- to 4-inch leaves that are toothed along the edges. The flowering stalk may surpass 12 inches in length. The rose-purple or lilac flowers, 1 inch or more in length, form a tubular corolla that is dilated upward. The staminode is not bearded, unusual for the genus. This species occurs wild in New Mexico and southern California.

Catalpa bignonioides *Walt.*
Indian Bean; Common Catalpa; Cigar Tree

Bignoniaceae
Bignonia Family

The bignonia family with 120 genera and 650 mostly tropical species are primarily American. The family has trees, shrubs, and extensive lianas. Except for ornamental species, the family has little economic importance.

There are eleven species of *Catalpa,* all native to eastern Asia, America, and the West Indies. They are deciduous, rarely evergreen. The leaves of most species have a disagreeable odor when damaged. The flowers are yellow, white, or pink and grow in large, showy bunches. Four or five species are cultivated.

Perhaps the most familiar bignoniaceous plant to Americans is the catalpa tree, a beautiful native of the New World. The tree may grow to a height of 50 feet and bear thousands of 2-inch-wide bell-shaped flowers that are white with two yellow stripes inside and dense brown-purple spotting. The fruit is a slender pod 6- to 15-inches long, the source of the common names Indian bean and cigar tree. In folk medicine the pods, seeds, and bark are believed to possess various therapeutic properties.

Jacaranda filicifolia *(Anders.) D. Don*
Fern Tree

Bignoniaceae
Bignonia Family

The American tropics has some 50 species of *Jacaranda*, trees and shrubs with showy tubular flowers in blue or violet borne in long clusters of panicles. Many botanists consider jacarandas the most beautiful trees. They are grown in warm or hot regions not only for their floral beauty but also for their delicately cut foliage. They are planted in parks and along streets, and some of the shrubby species make attractive flowering hedges.

Jacaranda filicifolia, native to Central America and northern South America, grows to a height of 60 feet or more and bears dense clusters of flowers of a deep violet-blue, each cup-shaped flower measuring 1½ inches in length and ½ inch in width. Their fragrance is strong and peculiarly distinctive. Both the technical species name, *filicifolia* ("fernlike leaves"), and the common name, fern tree, refer to the beautifully and finely divided leaves. It is very frequently planted as an ornamental.

Smithiantha fulgida *(Ortgies) Voss*
No common name known

Gesneriaceae
Gesneria Family

Gesneriaceae, one of the most important families in horticulture, includes herbs and a few shrubs and small trees. It is native to the tropics of both the New and Old Worlds. The family has some 2,000 species in 120 genera. Many species are hothouse plants and some, like the African violet (*Saintpaulia ionantha*), have become extremely popular. At least 10 genera have species that are horticultural favorites. Otherwise the family has no economic importance.

The eight species usually form scaly underground runners and propagate by these offshoots. The leaves are soft and usually heart-shaped, and the tubular flowers are red or yellowish blue. The several species of *Smithiantha* that are native to Mexico are herbs often sold in nurseries as gesnerias.

Smithiantha fulgida has flowers in terminal clusters that are mostly red but are sometimes yellowish. This species is commonly grown in greenhouses.

Sanchezia nobilis *Hook. fil.*
No common name known

Acanthaceae
Acanthus Family

A large family with many different biological types (climbers, bog plants, forest shrubs, xerophytes), the Acanthaceae has some 2,500 species in 250 genera. Most species are shrubs or herbs; there are a few trees. The family occurs primarily in the tropics of both hemispheres, but representatives are found in the United States, Australia, and the Mediterranean area. Except for the ornamentals, there are few species of economic value.

  Sanchezia has about 30 species of erect herbs or small shrubs that grow in the tropics of Peru, Ecuador, Colombia, and Brazil. The plants look lush with their large opposing leaves and heads or spikes of orange, red, or purplish flowers. It is often grown in greenhouses for its beautiful leaves, which are green with yellowish veins, and flowers. *Sanchezia nobilis,* native to Ecuador, is a stout shrub standing 3- to 12-feet tall with oblong-ovate leaves that are from 4- to 12-inches long. The beautiful flowers are borne in heads. Each blossom measures 2-inches long and has a yellow corolla with bright red bracts underneath the tube that are 1- to 1½-inches long. Several cultivars of this species have been developed.

Coffea arabica *L.*   Rubiaceae
Coffee   Madder Family

The Rubiaceae is an economically important family of plants, especially as a source of dyes and medicines. Quinine is an important medicinal member of the family, which has saved millions from malaria. With 6,000 species in 500 genera, it is one of the largest families of plants. It comprises trees, shrubs, and herbs, and grows worldwide, although mainly in the tropics.

Notwithstanding its scientific name, *Coffea arabica,* which is the source of 90 percent of the world's coffee, is native not to Arabia but to Abyssinia. Linnaeus realized, in giving the coffee plant its specific epithet, that the product was exported from Arabian ports.

Of the 25 species of *Coffea* only a few are the source of commercial coffee. *Coffea arabica* is a beautiful shrub that reaches up to 25 feet in height and has glossy leaves and clusters of excessively fragrant, white starlike flowers. The fruit, at first yellow, becomes red at maturity; it consists of a sweet pulp surrounding two seeds that are dried, roasted, and ground for the preparation of the berry for coffee. The sugar-rich pulp of the fruit originally was used in the preparation of a fermented beverage. It was the Persians who discovered the process of roasting the "beans," which frees the caffeine from a chemical combination with an acid, resulting in the preparation from which the beverage coffee is made. The stimulant effect of the beverage is due to the caffeine content (1 to 2 percent); the fragrance comes from an oil—caffeol—produced during roasting. The coffee plant, source of the most commercially important caffeine beverage, did not become common in Europe until the seventeenth century. Today, Brazil and Colombia are the principal sources of the world's coffee.

Luffa cylindrica (*L.*) *M. Roem.*
Vegetable Sponge

Cucurbitaceae
Gourd Family

The gourd family is of great importance as the source of edible fruits such as melons, squashes, pumpkins, cucumbers, and chayotes; some are poisonous; one species provides a hard-rind fruit used widely as a cup or dish. A number of members are grown for ornament. The Cucurbitaceae occurs in both hemispheres, most commonly in the tropics, and consists of 700 species in some 110 genera. It consists chiefly of climbing herbs of rapid growth.

Two species of *Luffa*—*L. cylindrica* and *L. acutangula*—are climbing cucumbers of the tropics with fruits containing a network of curled fibers that can be used as a substitute for bath sponges. When these fibers are extracted, they have some limited use in hat making, in washing and scouring operations, and in some types of oil filters.

Luffa cylindrica is now cultivated around the world, although it is native to the tropical parts of the Old World. It is of such ancient cultivation that it is no longer possible to state whether its native home was Asia or Africa.

Centaurea americana *Nutt.*
Basket Flower

Compositae
Sunflower Family

The composite or sunflower family is so named because the flowers are arranged on a common receptacle or disk called a head or a capitulum. Consequently, it is not correct to call the inflorescence of dahlias, asters, chrysanthemums, or other members of this family "flowers," as is commonly done, because the members of this family have heads composed of many flowers. The Compositae is the second largest family of plants with some 950 genera and some 18,000 species. It is cosmopolitan (although very rarely found in tropical rain forests) and grows in every conceivable habitat. Except for many ornamentals, the Compositae provide few economic plants: some become noxious weeds; a few are minor food and drug plants. This family is regarded as evolutionarily the most advanced of the dicotyledons.

The genus *Centaurea* comprises some 600 species and is native mostly to the Old World, occurring in Europe, northern India, and China, although there are some species that are native to temperate North and South America and one that is native to Australia. Many species are cultivated for their flowers. They are primarily annual or perennial herbs; occasionally they are shrubby. The flower heads are purple, blue, white, or yellow, often with appendaged or fringed bracts. A dozen or more species are cultivated.

The basket flower, or *Centaurea americana,* which grows from Missouri to Louisiana and Mexico, is a rather rough annual with stout stems, growing 24- to 72-inches tall. The round flowering heads, which may be purplish, rose-, or flesh-colored, measure 3 to 5 inches in width; there is a horticultural variety with white flowers.

105

Aster novae-angliae *L.*
New England Aster

Compositae
Sunflower Family

Aster comprises a group of temperate zone species (estimated to number 600) native to America, Eurasia, and Africa, but they are especially profuse in North America. A number of species are cultivated as autumn or late summer garden ornamentals: many annual garden "asters" do not belong to the genus *Aster* but are varieties of *Callistephus chinensis* (China aster).

The New England aster, which grows from Quebec to South Carolina and west to Colorado, is a perennial with stout stems reaching 3 to 5 inches in height and deep purple-blue ray flowers (commonly called "petals") that are ½- to ¾-inch long. There is a variety that has rose-purple rays.

Centaurea cyanus *L.*
Cornflower; Bachelor's Button; Bluebottle

Compositae
Sunflower Family

This species is native to southeastern Europe but becomes a weed in North America. A slender, branching annual, it may attain a height of 24 inches. The plant is woolly-white in the young stage. The blue, purple, pink, or whitish flowers are borne in thistlelike heads 1½ inches in width: the marginal (or outer) flowers are enlarged and fantastically fringed and curled.

Cichorium intybus *L.*   Compositae
Chicory; Succory   Sunflower Family

The nine species of *Cichorium* are annuals, biennials, or perennials native to Europe, the Mediterranean area, and Abyssinia. Branching conspicuously when in bloom, they usually have a deep, strong root system. The flowering heads are blue, purple, or white, each head having several to many flowers. There are two economic species in the genus: *C. intybus* and *C. endivia,* or endive; both have been cultivated for over 1,000 years but still look like wild plants.

The chicory plant is a stout, deeply taprooted perennial sometimes attaining a height of 72 inches. It is native to Europe, where it grows wild; in the United States it has escaped as a weed. The roots, which are the source of chicory, are roasted and ground and used as a substitute for or additive to coffee, giving the resulting beverage a bitter flavor. The flowering heads are normally deep azure blue, although in some strains, or races, they may be pink or white.

Cosmos diversifolius *Otto*
Rose Cosmos

Compositae
Sunflower Family

Our garden types of *Cosmos* are derived from a genus of some 25 showy herbs of tropical and subtropical America and the West Indies; most of the species are native to Mexico. They are late-flowering annuals or, in some cases, perennials. Recent work has created types of *Cosmos* that flower early and have a broad spectrum of colors. *Cosmos* has been adapted to cultivation in the more northern and cooler climates. Few garden plants have such delicate and refined flowers and bearing. The word *Cosmos* comes from the Greek, meaning orderliness, a thing of beauty.

A perennial with rather tuberous roots, although usually grown as an annual, *Cosmos diversifolius* attains a height of 36 inches with floral heads that are 2 to 3 inches in width. The ray flowers ("petals") are rose or violet; the disk flowers, yellow.

Dahlia pinnata *Cav.*
Garden Dahlia

Compositae
Sunflower Family

The 20 species of *Dahlia*, perennial herbs with tuberous roots, some of which are well appreciated for their large showy floral heads, are native to Mexico and Guatemala. The heads have yellow disk flowers and red, purple, pink, or white ray flowers. The dahlia was first discovered in 1519 by Cortez, the conqueror of Mexico, who found that it was already a long-established Aztec garden plant. A Spanish medical writer of the sixteenth century recorded that there were many colors of floral heads varying from white to shades of yellow, red, and purple.

Seeds were taken to Spain as early as 1789; these became the ancestors of some of the modern strains, or races, of *Dahlia*. By 1810, they were popular throughout northwestern Europe, especially in England, where they reached a height of enthusiasm that lasted until 1840, a phenomenon similar to that of the earlier tulip mania in Europe. In the early 1840s, when the potato blight hit Europe, many nurseries hoped that the dahlia tuber might be an acceptable substitute; but it never satisfied European culinary preferences. There is hardly a group of cultivated ornamentals with a greater diversity of strains, or races, or horticultural varieties than the dahlias.

Dahlia pinnata, the original species that was used to describe the genus, is a 48-inch-high plant with horizontal or somewhat nodding floral heads that measure 2- to 3-inches wide (but are greatly enlarged in the double forms of today).

111

Rudbeckia speciosa *Wenderoth*
Coneflower

Compositae
Sunflower Family

Rudbeckia, a genus of about 30 species of herbs, is native to North America. Some species are greatly prized as ornamentals for their showy inflorescences. They may be annuals, biennials, or perennials. The floral heads are striking, having large, yellow ray flowers, sometimes with a brownish base; the disk, or central portion, is greenish, yellowish, or purple-black. The famous and widely grown brown-eyed Susan (*R. triloba*) is perhaps the best-known species in our gardens and as a weed in our fields.

    Rudbeckia speciosa is a 36-inch-high perennial that grows from Pennsylvania to Michigan and down to Arkansas and Alabama; it has a beautiful floral head with twelve to twenty yellow ray flowers that are sometimes orange at the base, each measuring 1½-inches long; and the disk is deep purple-brown.

Solidago canadensis *L.*
Goldenrod

Compositae
Sunflower Family

This genus has approximately 125 species, mostly North American; there is one species native to Europe. Many species were introduced into England from North America at an early date. With their clusters of bright yellow flowering heads they form a conspicuous part of the landscape of northern North America (especially in the autumn). Goldenrods are generally considered to be weeds, but a few have become garden items. Modern cultivated varieties include Lemore, Golden Wings, Goldenmosa, and Lesdale. Several species, especially *S. leavenworthii*, were intensively investigated by Thomas Edison as a potential source of rubber: all species contain a white latex. The European *S. virgaurea* is called wound weed because of the former belief that it had healing properties.

The first species that was introduced into England (*Solidago canadensis*) was taken across the Atlantic from Virginia in 1648 by John Tradescant II. It has long stolons, or horizontal underground stems, that lead to easy proliferation. The plant may reach 60 inches in height. The flowering heads, borne in large panicles or clusters, are golden yellow and measure $1/12$- to $1/8$-inch long. The species grows wild from Newfoundland down to South Carolina and Texas.

GLOSSARY OF BOTANICAL TERMS

achene (akene): A small, dry, hard indehiscent fruit with a single seed in a single cell.

aerial root: A root that arises from the parts of the plant that are above ground.

alkaloid: A nitrogen-containing organic compound, usually with alkaline properties and marked physiological activity. Most alkaloids are found in plants.

ament: A long spike of unisexual flowers with scaly bracts; also called catkins.

anther: The usually saclike organ of the stamen that produces pollen.

arborescent: Treelike.

aril: An outgrowth of the attachment scar of a seed, often spongy, occasionally covering the entire seed.

aroid: A member of the aroid family or Araceae.

axil: The angle between a leaf and the stem.

bignoniaceous: Pertaining to the bignonia family.

bisexual: Having both stamens and carpels.

bract: A small leaf or scale, especially that below a flower or flower cluster.

bryophyte: A nonflowering plant such as moss or liverwort.

calyx: The sepals or outermost segments of the floral envelope.

capitulum: The cluster of flowers, especially in the composite family.

capsule: A dry dehiscent fruit with two or more carpels, often many-seeded.

carpel: The organ of a flower (usually considered to be a modified leaf) that encloses the ovule or ovules.

caryopsis: A seedlike fruit with a thin pericarp, or ovary wall, adhering to the seed; the fruit or "kernel" of grasses.

catkin: See *ament*.

chlorophyll: The nitrogenous, organic green coloring matter in plants involved in the capture of light in the photosynthetic process.

clone: The aggregate of the asexually reproduced progeny of a plant.

column: In orchids, the structure formed by the union of the style and stamens; in the mallow family, the tube formed by the union of the stamens.

convolvulaceous: Pertaining to the morning glory family.

corolla: The innermost set of floral segments, which either are separate or joined into a bell-shaped tube.

cryptogam: Belonging to the subkingdom of plants destitute of stamens, pistils, and true seeds.

cultigen: A plant known only from cultivation.

cultivar: A plant type known only in cultivation, not known in the wild; a cultivated strain (or race).

dehiscent: Splitting into distinct parts.

dicotyledon: An angiosperm (flowering plant) with an embryo that produces two seed leaves, or cotyledons.

digitate: Spreading like the fingers of a hand.

dioecious: Unisexual plants with the male (staminate) borne on one individual and the female (pistillate) on another.

disk flower: The tubular flowers produced in the central part (disk) of the floral head of the Compositae.

epiphyte: A plant growing on another plant or on some other object, for support or more light, but not parasitically.

essential oil: A volatile oil that is responsible for the odor of the plant; also called volatile oil or ethereal oil.

estrogenic: Referring to substances causing changes in

mammals during the estrus cycle.

evanescent: Perishing or disappearing early.

falls: The outer segment of flowers of the Iridaceae, often larger than the inner segments, frequently drooping.

family: In plant classification, a group of genera and species with common characteristics.

geniculate stamen: A stamen with its filament variously curved or abruptly bent.

genus: The natural group composed of distinct species.

glandular-punctate: Marked with very small dots, pits, or translucent spots owing to the presence of glands.

glochid: A barbed spine, hair, or bristle, especially one occurring on cactus plants.

gynandrium: An organ in which the male and female parts of the flower are united.

gynostegium: A complex organ originating from the union of the stamens and carpels in the Asclepiadaceae.

haft: The narrow basal part of the three outer segments of the iridaceous flower.

hallucinogen: A plant that may cause hallucinations or other mind alterations.

halophyte: A plant growing in a saline habitat, such as near the sea.

hybrid: The offspring of two genetically distinct genera, species, or varieties.

indehiscent: Not splitting into distinct parts.

inflorescence: A group or cluster of flowers.

intercalary meristem: A growing point that is not terminally placed on a stem but near the nodes.

iridaceous: Belonging to the iris family.

labellum: The upper (but, because of a twisting of its attachment, apparently the lower) petal of orchids, usually larger and very different in shape from the other two.

latex: A milky usually white fluid elaborated in specially differentiated cells of plants.

legume: A dehiscent fruit of one carpel, usually splitting along two valves; a pod.

limb: The expanded upper portion of a tubular flower.

lip: See *labellum.*

monocotyledon: An angiosperm (flowering plant) with an embryo that produces one seed leaf, or cotyledon.

monoecious: Having the stamens and the pistils in separate flowers on the same plant.

mycorrhiza: Certain fungi symbiotically associated with the roots of higher plants.

nectary: A region or organ of a plant that secretes nectar.

node: A joint on a stem where leaves or branches are attached.

obovate: Inversely ovate; ovate with the narrow end at the base.

oleaceous: Belonging to the olive family.

ovate: Egg-shaped, with the broader end at the base.

palmate: Shaped like a palm leaf with radiating parts diverging from a common base.

panicle: A long, loose inflorescence with irregularly compound branching.

papilionaceous: Belonging to the subfamily Papilionoideae of the pea family; having a butterfly-shaped flower.

pellucid-dotted: Spotted or pitted with clear, transparent dots.

peltate: Shield-shaped; attached by the under surface.

perianth: The floral envelope consisting of petals and sepals.

petal: The inner segment of the perianth, or floral envelope.

petiole: The stalk of a leaf.

phylogenetic: In accord with the evolutionary relationships of organisms.

pinnate: Having leaflets placed on each side of a common petiole.

pistil: The seed-producing organ of a flower, consisting, when complete, of ovary, stigma, and style; the female reproductive organ of a flower.

pollen: The fertilizing element of flowering plants: spores or grains produced in the anther.

pollinia: Masses of cohering pollen grains in the Asclepiadaceae and the Orchidaceae.

polymorphous: Of several forms.

pseudobulb: A thickened, bulbous above ground stem, from which leaves arise in the Orchidaceae.

radical leaves: Leaves arising from the root or basal portion of the stem.

ray flower: The outer, usually straplike, flowers of the floral head of Compositae.

receptacle: That part of the floral axis that supports the organs of the flower.

rhizome: A subterranean stem or branch that usually roots at the nodes.

rootstalk: See *rhizome.*

rosette: Clustered leaves arranged radially, often at ground level.

samara: An indehiscent winged fruit.

sapogenin: The nonsugar portion of certain compounds in plants called saponins.

saprophyte: A plant lacking chlorophyll that obtains its nutrients from decaying organic matter.

sclerenchyma: A tissue with thickened cell walls that gives support to a plant.

scorpioid inflorescence: A flowering stalk coiled like the tail of a scorpion.

sepal: One of the outer segments of the floral envelope that together form the calyx.

sheath: The tubular basal portion of (usually) a leaf that surrounds the stem or an organ.

spathe: A leaflike, usually colored, structure enveloping the inflorescence, especially in aroids and palms.

species: Individuals of the same ancestry and identical structure that pass on their characteristics unchanged from generation to generation; usually the smallest unit in plant classification.

stamen: The pollen-bearing organ of flowers.

staminode: A sterile stamen, nonfunctional and usually having morphological modifications.

standard: The large, upper petal of a papilionaceous flower; also the three inner, usually erect, sometimes arched, floral segments of iridaceous flowers.

steroidal: Containing a steroid, an active compound composed of four rings and seventeen carbon atoms.

stigma: The part of a pistil that is modified for the reception and germination of pollen.

stolon: A modified stem or runner growing along or under the ground and rooting at the nodes.

stone cells: Thick, hard-walled cells of the sclerenchyma.

strain: A permanent agricultural or horticultural variety; also called a race.

style: The elongated upper part of the carpel that bears the stigmas and through which the pollen tube grows.

subshrub: A plant almost, but not quite, attaining the status of shrub.

succulent: A juicy, fleshy, soft plant.

suture: A line of opening, a seam, or a dehiscence in dry fruits.

translator: An organ in the Asclepiadaceae and the Orchidaceae that effects the transfer of pollen.

tuber: A thick, usually underground stem.

undershrub: See *subshrub*.

variety: A subdivision of a species.

withy: Referring to a willow.

xerophyte: A plant capable of surviving in the driest of deserts.

zygomorphic: Irregular or unequal in shape.

INDEX TO THE PLATES

The common name of the flowers, where it exists, follows the Latin technical name in parentheses.

RICHARD EVANS SCHULTES, who has been the Director of the Botanical Museum at Harvard University since 1967, took his A.B., A.M., and Ph.D. degrees at Harvard, where he is also the Jeffrey Professor of Biology. The author of seven books and several hundred technical papers, Dr. Schultes is a member of the National Academy of Sciences (Washington, D.C.), the American Academy of Arts and Sciences (Boston), the Linnean Society (London), the Academies of Science of Colombia, Ecuador, and Argentina, and a Fellow of the American College of Neuropsychopharmacology. He has done field exploration or technical work in botanical institutions in Central and South America, England, Europe, and Asia. He was the editor of the international quarterly *Economic Botany* (1962–1979) and has been the editor of *Harvard Botanical Leaflets* (1955–the present).

WILLIAM A. DAVIS received a B.S. in Letters and Sciences and an A.M. in Applied Art from the University of Wisconsin at Madison. He has been a museum exhibits worker, a preparator of exhibits, and a free-lance illustrator of biology textbooks. Since 1969 Mr. Davis has been the Keeper of Scientific Exhibits, Botanical Museum, Harvard University, where he is also the purveyor of information about the glass flowers and the traveling chaperon for them.

HILLEL BURGER is the chief photographer at the Peabody Museum of Archaeology and Ethnology of Harvard University. His work—carefully balanced between objective presentation and aesthetic interpretation—has been extensively published in the professional literature as well as on the covers of art magazines and museum catalogues. His exhibition, "Interpretive Photography of Museum Objects," was shown at Harvard in 1977. Before coming to the United States, Mr. Burger worked for the Israel Museum in Jerusalem.

A NOTE ABOUT
THE PHOTOGRAPHS

The following equipment was used to photograph the glass flowers:

Camera	Sinar P. 4 × 5
Lenses	Kodak Commercial Ektar 8¼' f 6.3
	Schneider Kreuznach Symmar 300 mm
	Schneider Kreuznach Angulon 210 mm f 6.3
Film	Kodak Ektachrome Tungsten 4 × 5